Library of
Davidson College

THE
DIVINE INSPIRATION
OF HOLY SCRIPTURE

THE
DIVINE INSPIRATION
OF HOLY SCRIPTURE

WILLIAM J. ABRAHAM

OXFORD NEW YORK TORONTO MELBOURNE
OXFORD UNIVERSITY PRESS
1981

Oxford University Press, Walton Street, Oxford OX2 6DP
London Glasgow New York Toronto
Delhi Bombay Calcutta Madras Karachi
Kuala Lumpur Singapore Hong Kong Tokyo
Nairobi Dar es Salaam Cape Town
Melbourne Auckland

and associate companies in
Beirut Berlin Ibadan Mexico City

Published in the United States by
Oxford University Press, New York

© W. J. Abraham 1981

All rights reserved. No part of this publication may be reproduced, stored in a retrieval system, or transmitted, in any form or by any means, electronic, mechanical, photocopying, recording, or otherwise, without the prior permission of Oxford University Press

British Library Cataloguing in Publication Data
Abraham, William J.
The divine inspiration of Holy Scripture.
1. Bible – Inspiration
I. Title
220.1'3 BS480 80–41968
ISBN 0–19–826659–6

Typeset by Kings English
Typesetters, Cambridge
Printed in Great Britain
at the University Press, Oxford
by Eric Buckley
Printer to the University

To Muriel

ACKNOWLEDGEMENTS

THE author wishes to thank all those who encouraged and helped him in the work on this book. Fisher Humphreys, Patrick Roche, Robert Traina, A. Skevington Wood, and Basil Mitchell read various drafts of the material and gave extremely useful advice on both style and content. Very special thanks go to James Barr who gave invaluable encouragement and criticism. The blemishes and mistakes that remain despite all the help received are entirely my own.

A word of thanks too must go to Ronnie Rowe, Fay Deane, and Evelyn Rowe for the help they gave in preparing the manuscript for publication.

Bible quotations in this publication are taken from the Revised Standard Version of the Bible © 1946, 1952, 1957 and 1971 by the Division of Christian Education of the National Council of the Churches of Christ in the United States of America, and are used by permission.

CONTENTS

Introduction		1
1. The Deductive Approach		14
2. The Inductive Approach		39
3. The Concept of Inspiration		58
4. Divine Speaking and the Authority of Scripture		76
5. Exegetical Considerations		91
Postscript		109
Notes		119
Index		125

INTRODUCTION

THE point of departure for any contemporary analysis of divine inspiration must surely be the views of the last generation of Evangelicals. It is they who have kept the issue alive, have continually stressed its relevance and importance and have written most about this topic in recent times. Indeed I suspect that without them inspiration would have quietly disappeared from the vocabulary of modern Protestantism. And yet at once one is faced with a puzzle. Contemporary Evangelicals have themselves become less unanimous in their account of inspiration. The tradition which was articulated by B. B. Warfield in *The Inspiration and Authority of the Bible* and passed on by writers like J. I. Packer in *'Fundamentalism' and the Word of God* has not proved wholly satisfactory to those who would gladly identify with the Evangelical heritage in Christian theology. Of course the Evangelical position on inspiration has always had its critics. What is significant in the present context is that the standard line on inspiration has come under pressure from within the ranks of Evangelicals themselves.

It is no exaggeration to claim that contemporary Evangelical theology faces a crisis as regards its doctrine of inspiration. For some time it has been felt that its account has been inadequate. Much of this unease has been private and unpublished. Of late this unease has become sufficiently vocal and public to merit both attention and attack from some influential Evangelical circles. In America we have had Harold Lindsell's book, *Battle for the Bible*[1] while in Britain we have had the symposium by Jones, Andrews and Murray, *The Bible under Attack*.[2] The emotive tone of these titles and the discussion that has ensued are clear symptoms that all is far from well. There is indeed a serious crisis among Evangelicals regarding the doctrine of inspiration.

To many Evangelicals this is a profoundly disturbing event. They see the doctrine of inspiration as one of the key centres of unity that holds the diverse family of Evangelicals together. Their fear is that once that doctrine as traditionally held is dismantled or criticized from within then the doctrinal trust that has been built up over the years will be lost. Inspiration is a kind of bed-rock foundation. Changing the metaphor, we might say that it earns one a passport into the Evangelical tradition. It guarantees the general soundness of one's theological commitments; it is taken as a sign that one is committed to the fundamentals of the Christian faith. But once allegiance to inspiration seems in any way to waver, trust is liable to give away to fear and suspicion, mutual support is liable to give way to hostility and anger or perhaps sadness and pity.

The doctrine of inspiration held by many Evangelicals is reasonably well known. Unfortunately it has often been subject to caricature at the hands of its critics. But Evangelicals have themselves been diligent to correct the perpetual tendency to misrepresent their position by articulating their view as clearly as possible. In particular they have been intent in denying that they are committed to a theory of mechanical dictation or that they are committed to any kind of wooden literalism. This is very important, and it is a pity that these denials have been ignored by so many scholars. Their doctrine of inspiration can be stated very briefly, but it is a sophisticated doctrine none the less. Above all it must be seen as a serious theological proposal rather than a hermeneutical procedure, although it may well have serious implications for interpretation.

In the articulation of this proposal there has developed what might rightly be called a standard orthodoxy on inspiration. It enshrines at least three central ingredients which run as follows. The first is a claim about the nature of inspiration: inspiration is a unique act of God wherein the Bible was 'breathed out' by God in such a way as to become the very Word of God himself. The second is a claim about the *locus* of inspiration: inspiration properly understood applies only to the Bible as originally written down or given. The third is a claim about the implications of inspiration: inspiration involves or entails that the Bible is inerrant in what it says. We shall have much to say in due course about all these classical elements, but it is helpful at this point to say something about the first ingredient.

As it stands this first claim is reasonably clear. But Evangelicals have themselves taken great care to shield their position from ambiguity at this juncture. One useful way to reveal this is to outline the theories they self-consciously denied. There are at least four of these. One theory they vehemently denied was the theory of dictation. Another theory they denied is called the intuition theory. This view maintains that the biblical writers produced their works, not out of any special stimulation of the Holy Spirit, but simply by exercising certain gifts of religious insight or genius with which they were specially but naturally endowed. The prophets and apostles were simply men who were gifted to an unusual degree with the ability to discover and express religious truth. A third theory that was rejected is called the illumination theory. This theory emphasizes that the writers did receive a particular influence of the Holy Spirit at the time of writing, but this merely involved a heightening of stimulation of the abilities or powers already possessed. There was no communication of any new information. A fourth position denied has been labelled the 'dynamic theory'. Here the Holy Spirit is said to guide and control the writer in such a way and to such a degree that his thoughts were the very thoughts of God. In his selection of words to express the thoughts in writing, however, the writer had freedom of choice. So long as the words faithfully preserved the content of the thoughts that God had given him, then he could use what words he liked. All four of these views were denied by those who upheld the standard orthodoxy of the last generation, although there may have been a certain guarded tolerance as regards the last theory.

Over against these the general theory advocated is known as plenary or verbal inspiration. According to this view the work of the Holy Spirit is so delicate and sensitive that it even results in the choice of one word rather than another. There was to be sure the communication of ideas or thoughts, but these thoughts had to be expressed in words. Thus the guidance extended to the writers' choice of terminology; the words of the Bible are genuinely the very words of God. Hence this view is known as plenary or verbal inspiration.

To many this sounds very much like a theory of divine dictation. Evangelicals deny this abruptly. The distinction between the two is elaborated by drawing on the doctrine of providence. Rather than just dictate a message out of the blue to someone, God carefully guided events so that the biblical writers wrote down exactly what he desired. God had been at work from the writer's birth and even before that, preparing the way for his work. His birth into a given family, his exposure to particular cultural influences; these were no accident. His education, occupation, and experiences were all directed by the hand of God. Thus his ways of thinking and even his vocabulary and style of writing were the outcome of divine providence. By the time he came to write his particular portion of the Bible the very words he used were precisely the ones that God willed him to use, although there might be no clear consciousness that this was so at the time of writing.

We can see on reflection that this position is different from a theory of dictation. Two contrasts deserve mention. First, a dictation theory involves generally direct divine action in the world whereas this theory does not. According to the theory of verbal inspiration the action of God is concursive. Packer explains this helpfully as follows:

> We are to think of the Spirit's inspiring activity ... as ... concursive; that is, as exercised in, through, and by means of the writers' own activity, in such a way that their thinking and writing was *both* free and spontaneous *and* divinely elicited and controlled, and what they wrote was not only their own work but also God's work.[3]

Secondly, this position can genuinely accommodate differences in the style and character of the biblical writings. The stresses on the human side of the process of inspiration is sufficient to secure this. By contrast any theory of divine dictation cannot, for one would expect God to be uniform in his utterances to the biblical writers. Of course, one could never prove this but it is surely no accident that the principal objection to any theory of divine dictation is that it is incompatible with the variations of style, interests, outlook, etc. that exist in the Bible.

Introduction 5

It is this general account of inspiration that has been the foundation of the doctrine of Scripture for many Evangelicals in the recent past. They believe in verbal inspiration of the original autographs and they believe that this entails the inerrancy of the Bible. And yet despite its simplicity and sophistication it has failed to win the allegiance of all those who would gladly identify and support the Evangelical tradition within Christian theology. The reasons for this are many and varied. Some are unhappy that inspiration is confined or focused exclusively to the original autographs, especially since we do not possess these. Others feel that the theory involves a kind of sophisticated elaboration that goes far beyond the more moderate and less speculative teaching of the Bible itself on inspiration. Others are uneasy with the intellectualist and rationalistic tone of the theory as a whole. Perhaps it is the claim to inerrancy that has caused the most unease. Some have been tempted to jettison the term entirely, preferring the more ambiguous term 'infallible' as a substitute. Others have restricted the range of statements over which the term is to apply: it applies only to essential matters of faith and practice or only to what the Bible explicitly teaches rather than what it presumes or mentions. Yet others have tried valiantly to interpret the term in as wide a sense as possible. Despite this the term remains as an irreducible minimum for many.[4]

The key problem generated by the use of this term stems from the exacting demands of standard historical criticism. Nobody can brush aside historical study of the Bible these days. It is too well established as an academic discipline and too relevant to our recovery of the past to be ignored or rejected. Theologians, including Evangelical theologians, are initiated into their subject by means of it. History is simply indispensable; it is one of the key disciplines that is constitutive of academic theology today. But this poses a very serious problem for the person who is committed to inerrancy as a matter of theological principle. Historians are liable to find mistakes in their sources. They are liable as a matter of principle to arrive at an account of the past that differs from that given in the Bible. The claim that the Bible is inerrant will of necessity come into conflict with this. So a person committed to the standard orthodoxy of the last generation is faced with an acute dilemma. On the one hand his doctrine of inspiration commits him to believing that the Bible does not make mistakes even in matters of historical detail. On the other hand his commitment as a modern scholar and Christian to historical study pulls him in a radically different direction. It requires enormous sophistication to overcome this dilemma, and as we shall see there are a number of devices available to alleviate this tension. For the moment I simply want to draw attention to the fact that this dilemma constitutes one of the main pressure points for any doctrine of inspiration that involves inerrancy.

Despite this pressure it is instinctively felt by many that the doctrine of inspiration as outlined above is a *sine qua non* of Evangelical belief. It may even be felt that this is the only coherent account of the doctrine that does justice to what the Church has believed about inspiration for centuries. Anything less is too vague, *ad hoc* and obscurantist; anything less is an unacceptable departure from the traditional as well as Evangelical heritage. In due time I shall argue that it is high time that this claim was challenged, for it does scant justice to the diversity that has actually existed. However what is of particular interest at this point in our survey of the recent past is the obvious absence of any agreed alternative. Pressure on the doctrine of inspiration has not resulted in the development of a coherent and rounded doctrine of inspiration that would offer a positive and enriching account of what inspiration is.

The standard text-books in contemporary Anglo-American systematic theology have little if anything to say about our theme. Thus it is not disrespectful to say that what Professor John Macquarrie has written on this in his widely used *Principles of Christian Theology* (SCM, London, 1966) could be put on a postcard. On the whole the impression given in much modern theology is that the subject is of little importance or interest. Perhaps it is thought that even to show an interest in inspiration reveals a concern about matters wholly irrelevant to the intellectual needs and presuppositions of the modern age.

In Evangelical circles there is certainly interest in the

subject, but those dissatisfied with the standard orthodoxy of the recent past have little positive to offer in its place. This constitutes surely a most serious weakness in the thinking of those who would challenge the traditional view from within. Anyone concerned with the future of the Evangelical heritage in the next generation cannot be happy with this state of affairs. Destructive criticism that fails to generate a positive alternative is unhealthy, to say the least. Moreover it is pastorally irresponsible to leave the coming generation of students bereft of a coherent account of inspiration. Besides, inspiration is surely a key doctrine of the Christian tradition that has been dear to Evangelicals; to leave doubts as to what is to be said positively about it is to neglect a vital element of that tradition. Most importantly it will mean that those who are unhappy with the standard line on inspiration will be unwittingly aligned with those who reject inspiration entirely. They will be thought to tear up and destroy rather than deepen and enrich the Evangelical heritage. In the meantime people will continue to cling to the standard orthodoxy rather than tolerate a theological vacuum on inspiration.

This book is a modest attempt to offer a positive account of inspiration that is contemporary, coherent, and credible. It is written self-consciously from within the Evangelical tradition. I write from a perspective that cherishes the Evangelical heritage within which I came to faith. My forbears in this faith are men whose intelligence, sanctity, and evangelistic compassion continues to inform and inspire my spiritual and theological existence. Chief among these are John and Charles Wesley, Adam Clarke and Francis Asbury. In one sense I write out of a deep sense of loyalty to these men and to those who have kept alive their thought and emphasis. Indeed I think that neglect of the general approach to theology as a whole has led in some quarters to a serious misreading of what the Evangelical tradition was like in the past. This has set unnecessary and restrictive limits as to the shape and content of that tradition in the present. In other words, their way of expressing the Evangelical tradition that stretches back through Luther to the early Fathers and right back to the New Testament itself has been either ignored or muted in the recent developments of that tradition.⁵

Of course it has always been recognized that a genius like John Wesley has a place in the Evangelical hall of fame, but this is about as far as it goes; the real theological inspiration has been sought elsewhere. Not surprisingly this has had very serious consequences for the contemporary character of Evangelicalism. As a result the tradition has become excessively intolerant, if not bigoted in certain areas. It has lacked depth and profundity; it has lost its balance and a sense of proportion; it has ignored the riches and diversity of its own illustrious past. Above all it has fossilized its convictions and insights in the concepts and categories of the second half of the last century. This is generally the case with the whole ethos of the tradition. In many places there has been a loss of what Wesley and Whitefield cherished as the catholic spirit. A proper and entirely laudable concern for doctrine has degenerated into an exaggerated dogmatism. I am quite convinced that many Evangelicals are seeking to avoid this; they are recovering something of the depth and charity of their forbears. But there is still a long way to go, especially in regard to the approach to inspiration. Here the insistence on the categories of the late nineteenth century has been most evident. Thankfully these are now receiving extensive scrutiny but we are still at a loss as to what to put in their place. If this book can do something to identify and supply the great need that exists in this domain I shall be more than a little pleased.

My interest in this topic goes back to the days of my conversion. At first it was not a decisive or absorbing issue, for my reading of Wesley's sermons which first introduced me to theology ensured that my thinking centred on the broader themes of the faith. However, inspiration was never far from the horizons. At university it was often discussed in the circles in which I moved; for many it was the most important doctrinal issue. When I was in seminary in America it was very much a topic of debate, if not dispute, among both professors and students. It was while pursuing doctoral studies at Oxford that I first examined the matter with rigour. I was working in philosophical theology and my

Introduction

primary concerns rotated around the relation between traditional Christian claims about divine action in the world and the rational structure of critical historical investigation. As part of the preliminary work involved in this I looked at the concept of divine inspiration from various angles. For several reasons little of the research found its way into the final draft of my thesis, but it has remained as an issue that continues to haunt my theological reflection.

My basic contention is that we can have a more adequate account of inspiration than that which became standard orthodoxy in the last generation. My aim is therefore positive and constructive. I offer an analysis of inspiration that does best justice to the matrix of considerations that are constitutive to any discussion of this subject. It is on this ground that I commend it to the reader. That it is also intended as a contribution to the Evangelical heritage in Christian theology will make it of additional interest to some, but I must emphasize that this is a bonus which does not affect the truth of falsehood of my positive proposal. No doubt for some this extra dimension will be more of a hindrance than a help, for many react instinctively in a negative way to anything that is Evangelical. To this I can only reply that my primary loyalty is to the truth. It is in the interests of truth that I offer this positive review and account of inspiration.

Ancillary to this, however, I shall argue that the standard orthodoxy among the last generation of Evangelicals is much more innovative and unacceptable than many of its adherents and critics realize. There must be no blurring of the fact that Evangelicals cannot remain satisfied with the views of such key figures as Warfield and Packer. Much as is owed to them on various counts, we cannot remain content with their concepts and arguments. A new departure is both essential and possible. We need to review and revise what has been handed down from the past with thoroughness and integrity. Painful as this may be, it can no longer be postponed.

My general strategy is as follows. I shall begin by reviewing an early nineteenth-century theory of inspiration. By going back behind the orthodoxy handed down in the last generation, we shall be able to see how far that generation remains faithful to the tradition of its forbears. As one might expect there is both continuity and discontinuity. Both these are taken into account in the critique of what I have isolated above as the standard orthodoxy. One of my principal claims in this critique is that the latter tradition requires one of the central assumptions of the earlier tradition if it is to continue on the inerrancy of the Bible with any degree of plausibility. But this assumption is the one key element that the later tradition has itself vehemently and repeatedly rejected. In this chapter I shall also argue that attempts to relieve the tension generated by historical criticism are quite unsatisfactory. The end result is that one must either return to the earlier tradition and with it reject the principles and results of historical study, or one must seek to develop a different theory of inspiration. The latter is the only serious option open to us.

In the next chapter I examine the theory developed by William Sanday in *Inspiration,* his Bampton Lectures of 1893. Sanday is one of the few to examine our theme with a view to finding a position that would be compatible with serious historical investigation of the Bible. In this he deserves our attention, not least because he enabled a whole generation to live with this problem, although he himself failed to provide a satisfactory account of inspiration. Surprisingly, he continued to perpetuate the fundamental mistake that pervades the theories he sought to replace. Two other theologians who attempted to develop an account of inspiration that would be compatible with serious historical investigation of Scripture are H. Wheeler Robinson in *Inspiration and Revelation in the Old Testament* and James Barr in *The Bible in the Modern World.* They thus stand in the same tradition as Sanday. Unfortunately neither manage to provide an adequate account of inspiration.

It is this task that will detain us in chapter three. Here I outline and articulate the central ingredients of inspiration as it should be understood. This constitutes the heart of my positive proposal on inspiration. I shall sketch the basic meaning of the term inspiration, draw out the implication of this and defend it from some obvious objections. An

Introduction

objection that deserves extended treatment is the claim that I have left no unique place for the Bible in theology. This is taken up in chapter four where I argue that a key issue at this point is the issue of divine speaking, and not, as is generally supposed, the matter of inspiration.

By this stage we are ready to test out our suggestions about inspiration by the norm of Scripture. I shall argue that the position developed in chapter three makes much better sense of the classical texts of Scripture on this issue that does the theory of verbal inspiration. In virtue of this it deserves to be described as an entirely legitimate expression of the Evangelical tradition. In a postscript I shall take this one step further by arguing that my position is a continuation and restatement of some central elements in classical Evangelical thinking on inspiration.

There are three further points that should help the reader find his way through what follows. First, we should be aware that the arguments and concepts used in this study are at times delicate and subtle. The very nature of the issue makes this necessary. As is obvious to anyone who has thought about these matters there is no strict proof available for any theory of inspiration. And yet we can undoubtedly be persuaded that one option captures more of the truth and does greater justice to all the evidence than another. Therefore we should not be perturbed if the discussion ranges over several fields and if it takes time for the evidence to accumulate. Moreover some of the concepts involved require sensitive interpretation. So the reader must be patient and take time to digest and consider what is set before him. For example I refer to the classical theories of inspiration set forth in the next two chapters as being in turn deductive and inductive. For some these are technical terms that may seem out of place in our discussion. For others they have emotive overtones that may endanger understanding. In discussions of inspiration these two terms denote two different approaches to inspiration. A deductive type of theory begins with a basic theological claim about the meaning of inspiration and attempts to deduce from this what Scripture must be or contain. An inductive type of theory begins with Scripture as it is and attempts to arrive at a vision of inspiration that will be compatible with this. The former is often attractive to the systematic theologian while the latter is very attractive to the exegete or historian. The labels as they are developed and applied gather unfortunate connotations: a deductive theory is castigated as hyper-logical and rationalistic, while an inductive theory is criticized as loose and un-theological. This can easily confuse the issue and hide the merits and demerits of both kinds of theory. And yet they are still very useful concepts. They focus the general direction or character of a theory, help the reader to relate what is said to the history of discussion, and prompt us to find better ways to express the fundamental considerations that are relevant to the issue of inspiration.

Secondly, in the course of the discussion that follows I shall sometimes use the term 'Conservative Evangelical' to describe someone who is committed to the standard orthodoxy outlined above. I shall also use at times the term 'inerrantist' to describe the same position. It would be wonderful if I could avoid using any labels. Indeed the label 'Conservative Evangelical' is not without objection in the present context in that many take this simply as synonymous with the term 'Evangelical'.[6] But names and labels are inevitable so there is no point in complaining. In this book the term 'Conservative Evangelical' will be used to distinguish those Evangelicals who believe in the standard position from the growing number of Evangelicals who do not. It is decidely not a synonym for 'Evangelical'. Thus qualified it is perhaps one of the least emotive terms to use.

Thirdly, if I am correct in the analysis that follows it is imperative that future thinking on inspiration should clearly and resolutely distinguish inspiration from revelation. In my view this is vital if we are to rid ourselves of the confusion that reigns in this area at present. Readers therefore who are disappointed that I do not deal extensively with the topic of revelation should ask themselves if they have fully absorbed the arguments marshalled in this book. In my judgement the issue of revelation deserves to be taken separately from inspiration, and it is my intention to make known my considered opinion on this matter as early as possible. I hope that what little I have written on revelation will convince my critics that I do not for one moment undervalue the importance of this subject. For the present let us be content to make progress on inspiration.

1

THE DEDUCTIVE APPROACH

It was chiefly in the last century that the inspiration of the Bible became a burning and absorbing issue in theology. The issue that attracted the minds of many can be expressed as a problem about meaning. Theologians differed on how they should interpret the idea of inspiration, and these differences surfaced in the disagreements on what inspiration entailed and in the fine discriminations that were made in what it involved for the divinely inspired writer. No summary of the matter can improve on that provided by the celebrated Benjamin Jowett in 1861.

> The word inspiration has received more numerous gradations and distinctions of meaning than perhaps any other in the whole of theology. There is an inspiration of superintendence and an inspiration of suggestion; an inspiration that would have been consistent with the Apostle or Evangelist falling into error; and an inspiration which would have prevented him from erring; verbal organic inspiration by which the inspired person is the passive utterer of a Divine Word, and an inspiration which acts through the character of the sacred writer; there is an inspiration which absolutely communicates the fact to be revealed or statement to be made, and an inspiration which does not supercede the ordinary knowledge of human events; there is an inspiration which demands infallibility in matters of doctrine, but allows for mistakes in fact. Lastly there is a view of inspiration which recognises only its supernatural and prophetic character, and a view of inspiration which regards the Apostles and Evangelists as equally inspired in their writings and in their lives, and in both receiving the guidance of the Spirit of truth in a manner not different in kind but only in degree from ordinary Christians.[1]

Jowett not only reports succinctly the confusion that existed in his day, he also epitomizes the root cause of that confusion. Acquainted with the rise of critical scholarship, especially German scholarship, Jowett argued that the Bible should be studied like any other book. Today few would argue with this, for it enshrines insights that are invaluable if the riches of Scripture are to be identified and appropriated.

The Deductive Approach

The Christian today will, when he studies the Bible, rely on the canons of interpretation that are used for literature in general. In Jowett's day this was something new and disturbing. It was disturbing because scholars, in pursuing this ideal, arrived at conclusions that were clearly at variance with much traditional thinking about inspiration. To alleviate the tension thus generated there were two possible escape routes. Either one rejected the results of the scholarship of the day and the principles on which it was based and kept intact one's ideas about inspiration, or one accepted the results of scholarship and all that involved and made changes in one's ideas about inspiration. It is easy for the contemporary theologian to insist that the second of these choices is the only live option. The diversity of ideas that emerged when it was pursued is a compellng witness of the inherent difficulty of this course of action. Those who think that they can toss off their concept of inspiration in a few paragraphs would do well to ponder afresh the summary of Jowett.

Not surprisingly the great diversity of opinion was noticed by the watchful eye of B. B. Warfield, a key figure who gave to many the encouragement they needed to avoid this option entirely. He wrote sarcastically, 'Wherever five "advanced thinkers" assemble, at least six theories as to inspiration are likely to be ventilated'.[2] There is little doubt but that Warfield did more to shape recent Evangelical thinking on inspiration than any other theologian. During an illustrious career at Princeton he wrote extensively on the matter, and he is still read with enthusiasm in the present. Most of the arguments advanced by Conservative Evangelicals owe an enormous debt to his way of approaching the subject.

Ostensibly, Warfield approached the issue historically. As he saw it, all he was doing was articulating what the Church had always believed. Those who advanced a different account of inspiration openly neglected or repudiated the long-standing tradition of the past right back to the time of the apostles and Jesus. In place of the 'well-defined, stable doctrine of the Church', there was nothing but the 'numberless, discordant theories of inspiration' that vexed the agitated nineteenth century.[3]

This strand in Warfield's thinking finds a ready home in

the Evangelical mind. The past does matter to the Evangelical, for he identifies with a tradition that stretches back through figures like Wesley, Luther, and Augustine right back to Paul and the New Testament. There is therefore a real sense in which he cherishes tradition and does not lightly set it aside. Hence it is extremely tempting to follow Warfield and automatically reject what looks like innovation. This temptation must be resisted with some determination for at least two reasons. Firstly, outside the New Testament, the past is always of relative value. There is no guarantee that the Church is always correct. Anyone who takes the Reformation seriously must reckon with this. Secondly and more importantly, it is simply not the case that the Church has had an agreed account of inspiration throughout its past. Evangelicals must seriously face this. They must ask themselves if there is one theory of inspiration, not just within the Church's past, but even within their own past. There is far too much insensitivity to our heritage at this point. It is too readily taken for granted that the position taken by B. B. Warfield and passed into British Evangelicalism especially by J. I. Packer is the position of our forefathers in the faith. On the contrary, it is vital that we recognize that this position involves substantial innovations in theology. I am quite convinced that this is so, and my discovery of this was something of a disturbing revelation. In time it became the key factor that motivated me to work out an alternative account of inspiration that could legitimately be called Evangelical. In other words the historically relative nature of the views of Warfield and Packer fostered the conviction that the contemporary Evangelical had a duty to reassess the position taken up by our recent forbears.

Beneath Warfield's appeal to the past there is a much more significant factor in his thinking about inspiration, that of general approach. Warfield and the whole tradition he elaborates approached the issue of inspiration deductively. That is, they began with very firm convictions about the meaning of inspiration and from this they deduced by normal rules of inference what this entailed for the content and character of the Bible. From within this framework they

The Deductive Approach

then attempted to accommodate the results of direct, inductive study of the Bible as best they could. Where there was a strain between these two elements, that is between the deductions as to what Scripture must be like if it is truly inspired and between what Scripture seems to be like when it is studied like other literature, the former was given logical priority. The deductions ruled.

That there is strain in this strategy no one can or, for that matter, does deny. The strain comes, as we have seen, because of the claim to inerrancy. From divine inspiration Warfield deduced that the Bible is inerrant. When this clashed with the 'findings' of critical study, one remained committed to the former and abandoned the latter. The rule was well set forth by Augustine:

If you chance upon anything in Scripture that does not seem to be true, you must not conclude that the sacred writer made a mistake; rather your attitude should be: the manuscript is faulty, or the version is not accurate, or you yourself do not understand the matter.[4]

In this chapter I intend to examine this whole approach to the question of inspiration in some detail. At the outset, let me insist that I see nothing inherently wrong or theologically erroneous in such an approach. On the contrary, I consider it wholly appropriate for the simple reason that one can helpfully explore an idea by examining the consequences of its entailments. In other words, one can partially articulate what is meant by a particular concept by setting forth what can legitimately be deduced from that concept. So there is no inherent flaw in the procedures of the deductive approach to inspiration as such. Only obscurantists and those opposed to the use of logic in theology will want to take objection to it in principle.

The procedure, however, still needs to be scrutinized in practice. We must assure ourselves that it has been applied aright. More particularily, we need to assure ourselves of two things. Firstly, we must make sure that the foundation-idea from which the deductions are made is correct. We must be sure that the deductions are drawn from the idea of inspiration and not some other idea. Secondly, we must explore the strain that the whole approach generates when it comes face to face with the results of direct, inductive study of the Bible. We must make sure that the strain at this point is not unbearable. Both of these considerations will engage our attention in what follows.

A useful way to pursue these matters as they relate to the deductive approach to inspiration is to examine it from the side of history. Initially I shall go behind the standard orthodoxy outlined in the last chapter and look at a view of inspiration that preceded it. I shall show not only that the standard orthodoxy differs from a significant and influential earlier account of inspiration but also that a comparative study of the two throws great light on the quality of both as examined in the light of the two criteria just enunciated.

The theory I have in mind was developed by Louis Gaussen in a book entitled *Theopneustia: the Plenary Inspiration of the Holy Scriptures*.[5] Gaussen was Professor of Systematic Theology at Ovatoire, Geneva, and his book on inspiration was originally published in 1842. It was translated and published in England in 1888. C. H. Spurgeon's comment in the preface reveals its importance: '. . . it will be welcomed by the faithful, and it may confirm the wavering and win back honest minds from the fascination of modern theories'. What precisely did Gaussen believe about inspiration? Commenting on 2 Tim. 3: 16, he writes:

What they say, they tell us is theopneustic: Their book is from God. Whether they recite the mysteries of a past more ancient than creation, or those of a future more remote than the coming again of the Son of Man, or the eternal counsels of the Most High, or the secrets of man's hearts, or the deep things of God – whether they describe their own emotions, or relate what they remember or repeat contemporary narratives, or copy over genealogies, or make extracts from uninspired documents – their writing is inspired, their narratives are directed from above; it is always God who speaks, who relates, who ordains or reveals by their mouth.[6]

As a consequence the whole of Scripture, no matter what the subject-matter, is free from error. Indeed to acknowledge that there were erroneous statements and contradictions would be to renounce any attempt to maintain their plenary inspiration.

It is at this point that well-known difficulties arise. How are we to harmonize this claim with the Scriptures that we

The Deductive Approach

have to hand. A natural reading of the text of the Gospels, for example, must admit that there are discrepancies in the details of the accounts given. Few Evangelicals deny this and it is unnecessary to multiply examples. The Evangelical committed to inerrancy must, therefore, find some way of reconciling these facts with his theory. As I noted earlier it requires sophistication to do this well and convincingly. Without some device his position on inspiration is implausible, to say the least. One can think of several devices that might be called upon; let me mention two of the most popular.

One procedure is to play down the significance of any error. Charles Hodge expresses this charmingly as follows:

> The errors in matters of fact which skeptics search out bear no proportion to the whole. No sane man would deny that the Parthenon was built of marble, even if here and there a speck of sandstone should be detected in its structure. Not less unreasonable is it to deny the inspiration of such a book as the Bible, because one sacred writer says that on a given occasion twenty-four, and another says twenty-three thousand, men were slain. Surely a Christian may be allowed to tread such objections under his feet.[7]

Another procedure is to fasten on the distinction between the Bible and our interpretation of the Bible. In this case one reworks the interpretation of the Bible so as to make it accord with the settled facts, say of science. Again Hodge can be drawn on to illustrate this move.

> There is . . . a distinction to be made between the Bible and our interpretation. The latter may come into competition with settled facts; and then it must yield. Science has in many things taught the Church how to understand the Scriptures . . . It may cost the Church a severe struggle to give up one interpretation and adopt another, as it did in the seventeenth century, but no real evil need be apprehended. The Bible has stood, and still stands in the presence of the whole scientific world with its claims unshaken.[8]

In both these cases I find little to criticize severely. Hodge is correct to insist that the Bible must be read sensitively taking into account the settled facts of well-established study, and that when it is so read its contents stand secure. On the great cosmic questions about God and man and about salvation in Christ, there is a fundamental unity in the content of Scripture. Moreover, there is a ring of truth about that content that has stood the test of time, of critical study, and of experience. But this will not in itself dissolve the strain simply because the theory at hand insists on much more. It insists on complete and total inerrancy. Not surprisingly, therefore, other devices much more sophisticated and much less convincing have been developed. Let me examine two in some detail.

For one thing one can fasten on the distinction between a difficulty and an error. To say the Bible is inspired entails that it is inerrant. But that does not entail that one has shown that the Bible is inerrant inductively. The inductive evidence to hand might in fact suggest that there is an error here or there. But that is all it can do; it can suggest error. But suggested errors are not necessarily errors. As the claim to inerrancy rests on theological doctrine and not on inductive empirical evidence, we can live with this without undue tension. We know that once all the evidence is available then our faith in the inerrancy of Scripture will be vindicated. We know in the meantime that there is no error, only a difficulty, and difficulties do not involve a counter-argument to inerrancy in the way that errors would.

I shall comment on this shortly. For the present let us note that this procedure cuts very deep indeed, for it means that inductive considerations will never be allowed to count against the theory of verbal inspiration. Discrepancies, contradictions, inaccuracies, and anything else contrary to the theory will be skilfully redescribed to fit the theory. For this reason David H. Kelsey is correct when he suggests that the doctrine of verbal inspiration enjoys the status of a vast comprehensive hypothesis akin to the theory of evolution or the Copernican theory. In such a case 'anyone who relies on the hypothesis has the confidence that any conflicts that appear between facts and the hypothesis can be explained within the framework of the hypothesis'.[9]

The confidence of the inerrantist emerges particularly clearly in the field of hermeneutics. A theory of interpretation is consciously worked out to secure the compatibility of the phenomena with the theory. Here we need not concern ourselves with the fine details of the theory. What matters is its basic principle: essentially what it does is set up a collection of rules that will eliminate any interpretation that sees the biblical texts as erroneous or self-contradictory. The end result is a sophisticated interpretative apparatus which is a logical outcome of commitment to inerrancy.

The critic of the theory is likely to become bewildered at this juncture if he is not careful. If he really grasps what is happening, he will realize that the inerrantist has expertly sealed himself off from attack from the side of the text. There is no point in appealing to the phenomena in the text, for a fresh dispute will immediately break out on how the text is to be interpreted. By the time this is over, the critic will have discovered that the theory of inspiration under scrutiny is built into the foundations of the interpretative process. All this lends an air of unreality and depression to the whole discussion. The critic is wont to shake his head in despair while the inerrantist is likely to enjoy the look of disappointment in his critic's face. Victory seems to have been achieved once again.

This victory is hollow and empty. The inerrantist remains entirely self-consistent in his overall commitments but the problems he faces are no less genuine for being more subtle. The move to ward off criticism by developments in hermeneutics suffers from two major defects.

First, the hermeneutical principles developed are entirely *ad hoc*. They have no independent literary or exegetical evidence in their favour. They are made up to save the theory of inspiration from criticism and for no other reason. Not surprisingly, therefore, they are ignored or contravened when the theology of inspiration is being defended at other levels. Thus when Conservative Evangelicals argue that Jesus and the apostles believed in verbal inspiration it is taken for granted that any 'neutral' observer can see this from a plain and natural reading of the text. At this point one operates with a theory of interpretation that does not require the special *ad hoc* rules. Moreover, consider what happens when the ordinary reader complains that it is rather pointless to have a revelation written on inerrant but nonexistent autographs. He will be given assurance on two grounds. First, he will be told that textual criticism gives us the correct text; secondly he will be told that 'on the basis of the objective and public data of grammar and syntax and usage', we can arrive at the true meaning of Scripture.[10] At this level there is no mention of the rules that must be mastered later on; one gets the distinct impression that hermeneutics is a relatively straightforward affair. It is only at a later stage when the theory of verbal inspiration comes under attack from the side of the text that the additions are developed.

The second defect is of a theological nature. The great danger that attends this kind of interpretation is that it will corrupt the whole exegetical process. No doubt tempered with common sense it may prove harmless, but in the long term it will mean that Scripture must conform to preconceived convictions. The content of Scripture will be poured into a pre-set mould, and the highly sensitive task of listening to the whole range of the biblical data will be corrupted by a complex body of hermeneutical rules that are very deliberately developed to ensure that the theory of verbal inspiration can never be falsified by the content of Scripture itself. When this happens it is a serious matter for Evangelicals, for it means that Scripture is no longer being allowed to function as normative in their theology. Thus if they rightly grasp the issues at stake they should beware of the dangers that lie behind the enthusiasm to develop a theory of interpretation that is logically derived from inerrancy.

Thus far the inerrantist attempts to save his theory by trying to ensure that no interpretation of the Bible will admit anything contrary to the theory. In this he is working throughout on the level of the meaning of the text as it was originally intended. Normally when one has ascertained what an author intended to say one wants to know how far he is correct in what he says. For example, if a writer gives an account of a certain event in the past one will want to know how far his account is accurate and appropriate. In doing so one moves on to an entirely distinct level of investigation. One takes up what might be called the critical task. At this stage one evaluates the content of the writing according to various criteria depending on the nature of the actual writing before one. Inerrantists are equally intent on

The Deductive Approach

ensuring that this new phase of study will not come up with anything that would embarrass their theory of inspiration. At this level a very careful guard is set on the kind of criticism that can be applied to Scripture. Limits are built into the intellectual machinery that would find errors in Scripture. In essence this is the second major device that has been developed to keep intact the commitment to inerrancy.

It was this latter ploy that was adopted by Gaussen. In a discussion of the relation between criticism and divine inspiration, he enunciates two principles that are to guide reflection. First, criticism is to be a 'scientific' inquirer and not a judge. This permitted no less than the use of 'all the resources of your genius' to assure yourself of the canonicity and authenticity of the books of the Bible, but on completion of that, research was finished.

> ... when this work is over be steadfast. You have ascertained that the Bible is an authentic book, and that the unexceptionable seals of God Almighty are attached to it. You may hearken to what science and reason suggest, but you must listen to the voice of God; *sursum oculi, flexi poplites, sursum corda!* Fall down upon your knees! Lift up your hearts on high, with reverence, with profound humility! Then science and reason have no longer to adjudicate, but merely to receive evidence, no longer to pronounce, but to comprehend.[11]

Secondly, the critic is to be a historian but not a soothsayer. This permitted a study of the style, language, and circumstances of the writer, the date of his composition and the occasion of his writing. Beyond collecting such information one was not to proceed.

> But to proceed from that to crude hypothesis on the sacred writers, to make what they say depend on the haphazard of their circumstances, instead of considering their circumstances as prepared and willed by God for what they were to teach, to subordinate the nature, the abundance or the conciseness of their teachings to the concurrence, more or less fortuitous, of their ignorances or their recollections – this is to degrade inspiration, it is to forget that 'the men of God spake as they were moved by the Holy Ghost not with words which man's wisdom teacheth, but with those which the Holy Ghost teacheth' (1 Cor. 2: 13; 2 Peter 1: 21).[12]

This general policy of Gaussen is quite unacceptable. In broad terms it gives the impression that one is quite deliberately cooking the books in advance. Much more seriously it attempts to lay claim to being critical without really paying the price for this. It wants the benefit of sound historical scholarship without facing up to its demands. As I see it, it is wholly artificial and implausible to stop the historian from asking substantial evaluative questions about the content of the Bible. It is agreed that we can only read what Luke and John intended by relying on historical information about the date and circumstances of writing. But it is futile to think that the historian will stop when this is done. He will want to know how far Luke or John is reliable, and so will the Evangelical scholar. At this point evaluation of the content of Scripture is a wholly legitimate enquiry. But unless we will allow ourselves and the historian the possibility of finding Luke or John to be wrong, this whole complicated evaluative enterprise is empty and vacuous. We cannot tell the historian in advance of his study what results he can come up with. Gaussen, perhaps half-aware of this, defines, 'history' or 'historian' in such a way as to evade this issue. He does not admit its validity because he has loaded his concept of historian in such a way as to dismiss this central evaluative exercise as soothsaying. Such verbal manoeuvres are portentous nonsense. The historian must be allowed to ask critical questions about the historical content of the Bible, and if there are to be genuine questions we cannot presuppose in advance that he will always confirm what the Bible says.

Some contemporary Evangelical scholars face a very interesting dilemma at this point. On the one hand they want to be seen as taking history seriously; on the other, they do not want to admit the possibility of error. They are less likely therefore to be as heavy-handed as Gaussen in his strictures on historical criticism. This in part explains the emergence of the distinction between difficulties and errors. Such a distinction allows one to admit candidly that historians have found genuine difficulty in accepting that the Bible is inerrant. One might even say that historians have found what seem to be errors, but as a believer one regards these so-called errors as dificulties, rather than errors in any absolute sense. This is an honest position to maintain. It gives the critical process free reign but insists that the results

The Deductive Approach 25

of such criticism cannot be taken as the sole criterion of truth when it comes to the Bible. From a theological point of view it asserts that all such criticism can in principle supply is difficulties, but obviously those who reject verbal inspiration and inerrancy will be liable to treat difficulties as errors. However, the problem with this position is not that it is inconsistent. It is simply implausible. It means disregarding standards of evidence that are relied on in our normal lives. It involves waiting endlessly in the hope that new historical evidence will turn up to vindicate one's faith in the complete inerrancy of the Bible. One can of course hold out. But after a while this looks not so much wrong or impossible, but rather implausible, insensitive, and dogmatic. Therefore one can understand the urge to return to the kind of position advocated by Gaussen. The impetus for such a move comes in modern times from developments in the philosophy of history.

The exercise of critical historical judgement is an extremely complex affair. It would take me too far afield at this point to detail this here. Suffice it to say that it is widely recognized that one cannot exercise such judgement without resting on a whole network of presuppositions. It is to this fact that sophisticated restatements of Gaussen appeal. The general strategy at this point is to reject evaluation of the Bible that would call in question its inerrancy as subjective or supported by unbelief. Of course, claims by non-Evangelicals concerning the accuracy of Scripture will be welcomed with relief, if not triumph. But the impropriety of this is not generally recognized. All that matters is that the historian must not be allowed to report any errors. Once he does this, his claims to objectivity will be challenged. Historians who find errors cannot be objective because they do not have true presuppositions when they engage in criticism. The 'freedom' the historian boasts of is a false freedom: it is freedom in the flesh, a freedom sought by non-Christian believers. As Clark Pinnock puts it:

> Criticism must be squarely rooted within the Christian faith, and be aware of the Biblical self-attestation. The 'assured results' which are supposed to cripple infallibility are little more than the dubious assumption that Scripture may contain errors.[13]

What this amounts to is that the doctrine of inerrancy is written into the definition of history at the outset. This is an ingenious move, not least because it takes the whole issue back to one of presupposition, and this is a level where it is extremely difficult to overturn an argument. Presuppositions are by their nature rarely grounded on something else. They are part of the foundations of an argument rather than something one establishes by means of argument. Discussion at this level tends therefore to grind to a halt with either side convinced of victory. This is why they are ingenious and sophisticated in the extreme. The most one can hope to do is to show that the presuppositions are strained or implausible or that they have unacceptable consequences.

This is precisely the case as regards the move adopted by Pinnock. For one thing, to make his position look plausible Pinnock has to adopt a cavalier and insensitive attitude to modern critical scholarship. With all its variety, modern historical scholarship cannot be dismissed as a matter of 'chaotic flux and confusion'. Responsible and indeed believing historians who find it quite impossible on good inductive grounds to accept the inerrancy of the Bible cannot be dismissed in this manner. If one is to carry one's case with any degree of conviction, one must focus on the extremes of negative criticism, which has of course been daft at times, and then extend this view of it across the whole board. This, it seems to me, is what Pinnock has done. On the contrary I would maintain that any responsible historical criticism, whether professing to be Christian or not, must admit that the discrepancies that exist in the Gospels and elsewhere are genuine. They are not the product of unbelief or crooked presuppositions. They must be reckoned with in any Christian doctrine of Scripture.

Another objection to Pinnock's position is that it is inconsistent with the general strategy that he deploys in his apologetics. Pinnock belongs to an interesting wing of contemporary Evangelicalism that looks to history to warrant its claim. The initial appeal even for its doctrine of inerrancy is historical. It rests on what Christ is purported to have said about the Bible, this being established as a matter of historical scholarship. But if we take the present thesis

The Deductive Approach 27

seriously, this is a vacuous claim, for it is obvious that Pinnock is not talking about history as it is generally known and practised. He is talking about a special kind of history practised only by those who already believe in inerrancy. For him if history is to be truly critical it must be aware of what he has called 'Biblical self-attestation'. But this is just another way of insisting that the historian must accept that the Bible does not contain errors. Thus what was to be proved has been built into the discipline that was supposed to give some kind of proof for its truth. If Pinnock is to make out his case in the field of apologetics where he appeals to history then he must dismantle his claims about the character of critical history. He cannot appeal to history to support inerrancy if at the same time he insists that the historian must presuppose inerrancy.

By far the most serious objection to Pinnock, however, is that his retreat to a debate about the presuppositions of critical history is a last ditch effort to safeguard inerrancy. The contemporary debate about the presuppositions of critical history concerns matters which are much broader than Pinnock realizes. They concern questions about the rôle of natural law in historical judgement, about the nature of historical explanation, and about the possibility of the miraculous. They do not involve the question as to whether a historian should presuppose inerrancy or not. It is simply preposterous and question-begging to insist that a Christian historian must presuppose the inerrancy of Scripture when he examines the Bible. Narrow definitions of what a Christian is have been written into the whole enterprise of historical judgement in a way that is insensitive to the broad, complex, and dynamic rôle that presuppositions actually play. If a person does not recognize this then he is ill-equipped to make claims in the analytical philosophy of history.

The upshot of all this is that I do not think that Pinnock and Gaussen can maintain their position about inspiration and at the same time take history seriously. Moreover, contemporary devices such as the two examined are insufficient to cope with the emergence and results of inductive historical judgement. We must either abandon critical historical study and honestly admit this or we must abandon the theology of inerrancy. I think that we can and should do the latter. But before I explore this option, let us return to Gaussen and note the gap that divides Gaussen from the tradition that stems from Warfield. This you will recall was one of my central claims at the outset of this section.

The 'standard orthodoxy' in many Evangelical circles today differs significantly from Gaussen in two ways. First of all any mention of the original autographs is not to be found in his claims. In itself this may not be very important, for anyone who believes in inspiration will believe that the original autographs are inspired. What is significant however is that it makes nonsense of the claim that the 'standard orthodoxy' is entirely orthodox. There is a real break between Warfield and some of his predecessors, and we have accepted too readily his assurances to the contrary. The Princeton Theology of the late nineteenth century was far from being a simple restatement of the truths of historic Christianity. As Ernest R. Sandeen rightly argues, Princeton Theology was 'marked by doctrinal innovations and emphases which must not be confused with Apostolic Belief, Reformation Theology, or nineteenth century theology'.[14] This is true even of its view of inspiration which it strongly and persistently emphasizes applies to the original autographs only. But it differs also in an even more significant fashion.

When one reads contemporary Evangelical literature on inspiration, one hears constantly that inspiration is not dictation. When one reads Gaussen the identification of inspiration with dictation is unmistakable. Here there is a yawning gap between the two generations of scholarship. For my part, I must emphasize that Gaussen really did believe in dictation. The original shows this clearly:

... elle (L'écriture) est entièrement dictée par le Saint – Espirit, elle nous donne les propres paroles de Dieu, elle est entièrement (ἔνθεος et θεόπνευστος) donnée par le souffle de Dieu.[15]
... toute la partie des Ecritures appelée Prophetie, quelle qu'elle soit, a été complètement dictée de Dieu; en sorte que les mots memes, aussi bien que les pensées, y ont été donnés de lui.[16]

The Deductive Approach

The analogies that Gaussen uses bear this out. The writers are said to be 'the pens, hands and secretaries, of the Holy Ghost';[17] and he compares the relation of God to the writers of Scriptures to that between Racine and a village schoolmaster who writes out a drama at his dictation.[18]

Contemporary Evangelical scholarship must not be allowed to evade this fact. Attempts to minimize the difference by saying, as Packer does,[19] that this was a mere metaphor, are evasive and unhelpful. The fact is that prior to modern times many Christians really did believe that the Bible was dictated by God. This was nothing to be ashamed of in their times for they lived through a period when history as we know and practise it just did not exist. In its day the identification of inspiration with dictation was relatively harmless. It was simply part of the mental furniture of many of our forefathers. But the intellectual content and context of our times is different, and without in any way embracing passing fads and fashions we must come to terms with the use and results of responsible historical study. Indeed I would guess that it was a half-hearted effort to do this that led to the abandoning of the term 'dictation' and the emphasis on the original autographs. The sooner that we openly admit the fact of innovation within our heritage at this point the better. It will steel our critical faculties and prompt us to guard the resources of our faith by coming to terms in a responsible manner with the knowledge that was not available to our forefathers. Above all it will save us from imprisoning the Evangelical heritage in the categories of the late nineteenth century as developed at Princeton.

Two facts have now been established. First, the standard orthodoxy is not a simple restatement of the view of inspiration that was prevalent in Evangelical circles prior to the late nineteenth century. On the contrary it involves considerable revision. Secondly, like its predecessor it involves enormous strain when it comes into contact with inductive study of the text. Indeed the strain is too great for any reasonable person to want to bear. So, we must either abandon the theology of inerrancy or we must abandon a natural and honest study of the Bible. The first option is the only serious one of the two. But if we abandon inerrancy must we also abandon inspiration? That is the issue we must now face.

This question takes us to the core of the standard orthodoxy, for it raises the other question I suggested was vital in our examination of the deductive approach as developed by Conservative Evangelicals. If we find that inerrancy is not deduced from inspiration but is really deduced from some other concept then the idea of inspiration remains secure from attack. But which is it? I suggest that it is not deduced from inspiration at all. Let me explain.

Suppose we ask very generally what it is that generates a doctrine of inerrancy. On what grounds do we establish that the Bible is inerrant? Evangelicals offer an array of arguments at this point, of which the major, classical, arguments are four. Inerrancy is required by the teaching of Jesus, by the teaching of Scripture as a whole, by the very idea of inspiration itself, and by the idea of biblical authority.

In reporting this I am not denying that pastoral considerations often play an enormous role in the commitment to inerrancy. I have come across many Evangelical scholars who have very serious misgivings about the standard orthodoxy but who find it very difficult to abandon the position they have inherited from the recent past. Some feel that abandoning inerrancy would open the floodgate to a whole host of critical problems that they are reluctant to face. More often they feel that any alternative would be too complicated for the beginning student or the average layman to digest. One can sympathize with the sense of pastoral care that this represents, but one cannot applaud it unreservedly. Such an attitude both overestimates and underestimates.

On the one hand it overestimates the problems generated by critical study. To be sure, critical scholarship does now and then get out of hand, and it can become a kind of cult that would easily divert one from the central message of the Bible. However, the answer to this is not to reject critical scholarship in a fit of alarm but to draw judiciously on every available insight that will bring to us the great riches that the Bible contains. Students and laymen will respond to this if it is done with care and sensitivity. On the other hand this attitude of reticence towards alternative accounts of

The Deductive Approach

inspiration completely fails to acknowledge how sophisticated and complicated the standard orthodoxy has now become. Even yet the process of formulation and development is incomplete, for it is openly recognized that aspects of the theory of verbal inspiration still require attention. The fact is that the standard orthodoxy is a highly complex theory and it is far from easy to initiate the beginning student into its many nooks and crannies. Those who still cling to it for pastoral reasons must reckon with this more realistically than they have to date. Above all they must acknowledge that pastoral considerations are secondary compared to the philosophical and theological commitments related to verbal inspiration. In other words what really matters is the group of four arguments mentioned above.

We should note two things about these arguments. First, they implicitly recognize that the case for inerrancy does not rest on either direct exegesis of biblical texts or on direct inductive evidence. Nowhere does the Bible speak of inerrancy. All sides in the debate accept this, as they must. At best inerrancy is an inference from texts that make no reference to the concept. So it is not a matter of exegesis. Nor is it a question to be decided by accumulating inductive evidence. Thus no one has shown the Bible to be inerrant by going through its pages and proving it contains no mistakes. The very idea is impractical, for the complete and exhaustive evidence that this requires is not available. Secondly, the four arguments used reduce in the end to two. The argument from the teaching of Jesus and the argument from the teaching of Scripture in general are essentially ones which support the argument from inspiration. It is because Jesus and Scripture in general teach verbal inspiration that we are required to believe in verbal inspiration and it is because we thus believe that we are required to believe in inerrancy. This makes the argument from inspiration the key one of the four. To this we add the argument from authority, an argument that enjoys an entirely independent pedigree from the others mentioned. Let us look at it briefly before we inspect the argument from inspiration.

The argument from authority enjoys an ambivalent status among Evangelicals. It ranks as a philosophical or linguistic argument about the concept of authority, and due to the widespread influence of Barth, many Evangelicals are very uneasy with such arguments. Generally Evangelicals like to rely entirely on Scripture alone in their apologetic, although the literature on inspiration reveals how difficult it is to live up to this ideal in practice. The argument can be put nicely thus: no truth-loving person can agree to accept any document as both authoritative and false; Evangelicals accept the Bible as authoritative; therefore, they cannot accept any part of it to be false. Evangelicals press this argument especially forcefully on their fellow-Evangelicals. Alas, it is quite inadequate. It only has plausibility if one fails to specify the scope of the authority of Scripture. When we do this the argument collapses. Thus it is entirely consistent to say that the Bible is authoritative in matters of faith and practice but may be false, for example in geographical or historical detail. If it errs in matters that are not germane to its primary spiritual intent, this is quite irrelevant to its being trustworthy in the central matters of the faith. The argument from authority simply overlooks this, or so qualifies the concept that it begs the question from the outset.[20]

The really important question can now be restated and examined. Given that the main argument for inerrancy is that it is an inference from divine inspiration, is this inference valid? Can we deduce inerrancy from inspiration? Conservative Evangelicals are convinced that it is entirely valid to do so. I simply do not see this as true. Indeed in due course I shall argue that a disciplined analysis of the idea of inspiration cannot be used to defend inerrancy. In the absence of such an analysis it is difficult to disprove conclusively the contrary position. Inevitably the 'neutral' observer will feel that opponents in the debate reach here a kind of rock-bottom, intuitive judgement that is not amenable to further argument. One side thinks that inspiration guarantees inerrancy, the other does not, and that is the end of the matter.

Tempting as it is to adopt this position, it is premature when one reflects more carefully on a comparison between the standard orthodoxy and the theory propounded by Gaussen. Consider for a moment why Gaussen believed in

The Deductive Approach

inerrancy. There can be little doubt but that his belief in inerrancy was a consequence of his belief in divine dictation. The argument in the case of dictation is relatively simple. Given certain assumptions about God (that He is omniscient and morally good, for example) it is not difficult to generate a doctrine of inerrancy. Thus from the proposition that all that God dictates is free from error and the proposition that the Bible is dictated by God, we can infer that the Bible is free from error. Even if we have doubts about certain aspects of this argument, we can be certain that it was some such inference as this that was the foundation of Gaussen's belief in inerrancy.

At this point Gaussen is repeating an argument that has a long history in Christian thought but which is often expressed in different terms. It is more common to find it couched in terms of divine speaking rather than in terms of divine dictation. Thus Irenaeus writing in AD 177 argued: 'The scriptures are perfect because uttered by the Word of God, and His Spirit.'[21] Clement of Rome in AD 91 put it even more simply: 'The scriptures are true utterances of the Holy Spirit.'[22] These claims are self-evidently true. It is indeed the case that if God utters a proposition, then that proposition is true. An omniscient agent such as God just does not make mistakes. Gaussen and many of those before him who believed in inerrancy were entirely consistent in their commitments. If you believe in dictation then, other things considered, you must believe in inerrancy.

Gaussen was led into the identification of inspiration and dictation and thereby to inerrancy by a smooth path. In his attempt to establish that Scripture is divinely inspired, there is the usual appeal to the classical proof-texts of the New Testament. But the weight of the argument falls on the claim of the prophets in the Old Testament to be proclaiming a word from God. This is then extended from the prophets to cover the record in which their word is embedded, i.e., the whole of the Old Testament, and extended to cover the New Testament by treating the apostles as on a par with the prophets. To be sure, there is also the appeal to the supposed attitude of Jesus to the Old Testament, but the emphasis does not rest there on the whole. If the weight of the argument is cast on the claim of the prophets as extended to the whole of Scripture, it is a minor move from that to dictation. For what is dictation but speaking, albeit in a slow manner to a secretary and for restricted purposes. And the claim of the prophets, according to Gaussen, is that they were spoken to by God. As they constituted the primary sources for inspiration, it is plausible to see Gaussen's account of them as the source of his identifying inspiration with dictation. Indeed we can appeal to no less an authority than Warfield for this understanding of the prophets.

> The process of relevation through the prophets was a process by which Jehovah put his words in the mouths of the prophets, and the prophets spoke precisely these words and no other. So the prophets themselves ever asserted . . .
> . . . It is a process nothing other than 'dictation' which is thus described (2 Sam. 14: 3, 19), though of course, the question may remain open of the exact processes by which this dictation is accomplished.[23]

But what if dictation is abandoned? Once this goes I suggest that the commitment to inerrancy must go as well. Without dictation inerrancy is without warrant, for the two are linked by way of logical inference. Dictation is the foundation from which the claim to inerrancy flows; it does not flow from inspiration unless the two are confused as they are by Gaussen. If I am correct in this then we must face the possibility that claims to inerrancy trade on an older tradition whose categories have been openly rejected. Thus the dispute about the relation between dictation and inspiration is far from being an aside about the mechanics of inspiration. It takes us to one of the most serious problems in recent Evangelical thought on inspiration. What I am suggesting is that the claim to inerrancy really rests on a covert appeal to the concept of dictation, which despite disclaimers to the contrary, is still basic to the thought of those who continue to insist that inspiration means or guarantees inerrancy. They have abandoned use of the term 'dictation', and may thus sincerely avow that inspiration is not to be confused with dictation. But in substance that is what they mean, for there is no other relevant way in which divine inspiration can be seen to license inerrancy. Those who regard the issue of

The Deductive Approach 35

dictation as a matter of the mechanics of inspiration only mask this informal assimilation of inspiration to dictation.

It is of great importance that the exact nature of the above claim be recognized. Let me repeat that I am not saying that there is any overt commitment to dictation. Clearly there is not. Recent Evangelical literature has insisted that dictation is not a live option in any responsible account of Scripture. Nor am I saying that dictation is the one and only possible warrant for a doctrine of inerrancy, for it would not be difficult to think of other divine acts that would generate this position. Thus if one could somehow show that all of the Bible was miraculously written by the finger of God then this too would license the claim that there were no errors in Scripture. My point is that dictation is the only relevant assumption to look to as an explanation for the commitment of Evangelicals to inerrancy. This explanation is essentially historical in character. It suggests that Conservative Evangelicals took the doctrine of inerrancy from a theological tradition that based its convictions on a doctrine of dictation. Historically, therefore, Conservative Evangelicals cannot evade the fact that their own position rests indirectly on an appeal to divine dictation. To reject this is to reject the foundations of their theology of inerrancy. The foundations could, of course, have been otherwise, and do not of necessity involve dictation. But in the context and historical circumstances out of which the contemporary emphasis on inerrancy emerged the foundations do in actual fact involve dictation. Thus it is in order to suggest that the claim to inerrancy rests on a covert appeal to dictation.

Two considerations go a long way to bear this out. First, a general reading of the literature reveals that in the discussion of inerrancy there is a strong tendency to confuse divine inspiration with divine speaking and related concepts. It is no accident that the quotations from Irenaeus and Clement are favourites with Conservative Evangelicals as they seek to defend inerrancy. This tradition is reflected very clearly in the arguments of those who speak of God being the author of Scripture in an unqualified way and from this deduce that it cannot contain errors. It is also no accident that in the same literature it is invariably pointed out that such expressions as 'Thus says the Lord' or 'The Lord said' occur 1,904 times in the Bible.[24] This is part of a general strategy which in essence uses arguments that depend upon divine dictation and divine speaking rather than divine inspiration to support inerrancy. At the very least they help to soften up the reader to receive the doctrine of inerrancy. Such moves depend for their validity upon the kind of theory articulated by Gaussen.

Secondly, it is clear that the urge to defend inerrancy at all cost works its way back into the very notion of inspiration that is developed by theologians like Warfield. There is indeed a gap between those committed to verbal inspiration and the theory of Gaussen, but the gap must be identified and marked off with care. Warfield and those who followed him have very definitely abandoned the term 'dictation'. At this point we must accept their avowals. And yet the logical connection between inerrancy and dictation takes its revenge, as it were, in their formulation of what inspiration is. They cannot use the term 'dictation' but they must provide an act of God or a set of acts of God that will bring about the exact results that dictation does. I think that this has happened and the difference between the two views is just one of terminology. What we are in fact offered is a kind of telepathic dictation without the writer being aware of it. Some confirmation for my claim comes from the following summary of verbal inspiration as it is stated by Millard Erickson.

> Here is how the new evangelicals conceive of verbal inspiration. God has worked in the life of the apostle or prophet, making him the kind of person that he is, possessing the vocabulary that God wanted him to have. The man lives in such close relationship to God as to be very sensitive to his working. Then God through the Holy Spirit, moves in his mind, directing and creating thoughts, and in a very precise fashion. *So the man writes, using the words that God would have him use, yet without any consciousness of dictation.*[25]

It is very revealing that Erickson can slip unconsciously into talk about dictation. The fact is that the 'new evangelicals' he describes are stalwart defenders of inerrancy. The highly complicated process of divine activity they have invented to underwrite this may be called 'verbal inspiration'

The Deductive Approach

but in reality it is more akin to divine speaking and divine dictating than it is to divine inspiration. No less a figure than Packer gives ample evidence of this fact: 'The Bible is inspired in the sense of being word-for-word God-given.'[26] He even half-suggests that the analogy with dictation has its merits when it is understood figuratively. Taken figuratively it means that 'the authors wrote word for word what God intended.'[27] This whole emphasis on words is a carry-over from a dictation theory. Packer has rejected the term but the whole idea lives on to take on a fresh life under the auspices of his theory of inspiration. In that theory inspiration continues to be approached as if it were some kind of complicated speech-act of God.

This is the fundamental problem in classical deductive approaches to inspiration. It is not that proponents of such theories are wrong to try and draw valid inferences from the idea of inspiration. In this they are correct. It is rather that they have invariably been working less with the concept of inspiration than with the concept of divine speaking. Surely it is harmful and confusing to approach divine inspiration from this angle. Any responsible and coherent account of inspiration must at least begin with the possibility that there is as much difference between divine inspiration and divine speaking as there is between human inspiration and human speaking. It must consider as a live option that divine inspiration is a basic act or activity of God that is not reducible to other divine acts or activity. It must not be confused with other activity of God, whether this be the creative activity of God or the speaking activity of God. Yet Gaussen's account ignores this vital point. He never pauses to reflect on how such a predicate as 'inspire' should be interpreted. He never stops to question whether the fundamental models he relies on to give content to the concept of inspiration are appropriate. He never halts to examine the analogies that inform his thinking about inspiration.

In this he is not altogether at fault. It is only in our very recent past that we have become aware and self-conscious about the importance of such conceptual analysis. It is especially important in theology, for God is not a part of the physical universe, and much of our language has been developed for application to natural entities and agents. When they are predicated of God we must be cautious and qualify our concepts and their applications. Gaussen simply could not have grasped the significance of this, so we must be charitable in our final estimate. But we must equally avoid his errors and re-route the whole discussion on inspiration into more adequate channels.

As we shall see when we turn to exegesis there are biblical reasons for pursuing such a course. For the present we can report that we have found two good grounds for taking such action. On the other hand the standard orthodoxy is too close a relation to a theory of divine dictation for one to be entirely comfortable. Certainly it is not a theory of dictation in any formal sense, but it does seem to have developed in order to safeguard the doctrine of inerrancy, and that most certainly is linked by inference to dictation. On the other hand we have discovered that the standard orthodoxy cannot adopt in any natural way the results of an elementary study of the Bible. The facts revealed by an inductive study of the text of Scripture cannot be ignored in any account of inspiration that seeks to be comprehensive. We must deal with the Bible that is before us and we must face up to what is clear to those who read it with reverence and care. As Charles Hodge put it succinctly many years ago: 'Our views of inspiration must be determined by the phenomena of the Bible as well as by its didactic statements.'[28]

2

THE INDUCTIVE APPROACH

THE standard account of inspiration provided by the last generation of Evangelicals was a revision of an earlier and different theory of inspiration. That revision is open to two sorts of objection that render it untenable. First, it requires the assumption of dictation (or some act of God very much like dictation) to keep intact the claim that the Bible is inerrant. Without this one essential ingredient the standard account is without foundation. Secondly, the claim to inerrancy cannot itself be maintained without there being unbearable strain. It cannot have a comfortable life alongside either the nature or results of responsible and indispensable historical study of the Bible. The common devices relied on to alleviate this strain are unacceptable and unrealistic.

Yet the attempt to revise was in principle correct. Theology is not a static discipline; it must take into account such new information and insights as were unavailable to our forefathers. In particular, the insistence that any theory that involves dictation is inadequate hardly needs to be justified. The avowals of the last generation to abandon or reject this concept must be reaffirmed, although we need to be more watchful than our predecessors in this respect. Moreover, we cannot turn our backs on the riches that history has brought to our faith. Here again the last generation was right to insist that history cannot be shunned, although we may question if they were always or fully prepared to acknowledge what this involved. What we need to do in the present is to move beyond the revisions of the past and incorporate both these convictions in a positive analysis of inspiration.

Before we proceed to this I want to examine what has been called the inductive approach to inspiration. The basic intent of this is to secure an account of inspiration that will be compatible with the actual phenomena of Scripture.

To be sure, no one is prepared to ignore entirely the phenomena of Scripture. Thus those committed to the deductive stance insist that inspiration does not preclude the writer developing his own literary style or making use of written sources. Indeed it is inductive considerations such as these that have led Evangelicals to reject any 'mechanical' notion of inspiration. The issue at this point is one of degree. How far will one go in giving due recognition to inductive considerations? Will discrepancies, contradictions, and inaccuracies be allowed to count as part of the phenomena of the Bible? Inerrantists generally dispose of this issue by developing a set of procedures that will make it look as if the Bible does not contain such things. The very existence of these procedures brings to light how important inductive considerations have become in contemporary thinking about inspiration. Even if the ultimate aim is to ignore such considerations, one has to set forth and defend an apparatus by means of which one can ignore them. One cannot simply proceed as if there were no problems to be faced. Inerrantists therefore set a careful guard on the whole interpretative and critical process. Only those interpretations and evaluations of the text that harmonize with the theory of verbal inspiration will be allowed to rank as appropriate. All others will be rejected as invalid.

It is precisely this move that those committed to an inductive approach to inspiration repudiate. Generally they work from the opposite direction. For them, any theory of inspiration that assumes inerrancy must be false for it fails to reckon with the Bible as we know it when it is examined like any other book. Thus they consciously attempt to work out a position on inspiration that will accomodate the results of inductive study. They begin with the phenomena of the Bible and construct a theory that will harmonize with them. Let us explore in some detail what fruits such a course produces.

We shall do this initially by focusing on the account of inspiration furnished by William Sanday of Oxford. Sanday set forth his ideas on inspiration in the Bampton Lectures of

The Inductive Approach

1893.[1] They are a model of well-informed and concise theological prose. They quickly became something of a bestseller, passing through three editions in three years.

In contrast to Gaussen, Sanday is determined to take seriously the application of historical criticism to the Bible. Much of his Bampton Lectures is thus devoted to a treatment of the historical genesis of the biblical literature, i.e. to questions of date, composition, background, authenticity, historical trustworthiness, etc. Interlaced with this is an account of the doctrinal development wherein the literature is accepted as the canon of the Church and viewed as a divinely inspired corpus. It is no surprise, therefore, that Sanday desired to develop a conception of inspiration that he designates as inductive or critical. Both these terms suggest a readiness to arrive at a view of inspiration that is compatible with an honest and searching study of the literature as it stands. For Sanday the Bible must be studied like any other book; it would be hopeless to try and stop such investigation even if it were right to do so.

Allowing that the Bible was to be studied like any other book did not sanction the assumption that it must be like any other book. Although this assumption had consciously or unconsciously influenced many, it was premature.

> Let us by all means study it if we will like any other book, but do not let us beg the question that it must be wholly like any other book, that there is nothing in it distinctive and unique. Let us give a fair and patient hearing to the facts as they come before us, whether they be old or whether they be new.[2]

Such a hearing would reveal that the books of the Bible 'speak with no uncertain sound in their claim to a real divine inspiration'.[3] Foremost in this regard were the prophets and apostles.

> The distinguishing characteristic of the prophets, first of their speech and action and afterwards of their writings, was the firm and unwavering belief that they were instruments and organs of the Most High, and that the thoughts that arose in their minds about Him and His will, and the commands and exhortations which they issued in His Name, really came at His prompting, and were really invested with His authority.[4]
> With one consent they would say that the thoughts which arose in their hearts and the words which arose to their lips were put there by God.[5]

Sanday considered this account of the prophets and apostles to be correct. In a real objective sense, God had given to them special revelation. His reasons for accepting this are many and varied. Not only did such a claim harmonize with a theistic world-view that was itself supported by natural theology, it also fitted in with the following phenomena: the strong assurance and testimony of the prophets themselves; the general recognition of the claim by their contemporaries; the remarkable consistency in a long line of prophets, not easily compatible with hallucination; the difficulty of accounting for the prophets' teaching as the product of ordinary causes, whether in the prophets themselves, their race, or the constitution of the human mind; the immense permanent significance and value of the prophetic teaching.

The prophets and apostles constitute the prime example of divine inspiration. In them 'not only the fact of Inspiration but the manner of it are most evident'.[6] It is they who let us see the workings of inspiration and represent the typical expression of the divine element in the Bible.

However, around this nucleus of primary inspiration there gathered a sort of secondary inspiration. The primary revelation received by prophets had to be recognized by acts of worship and praise and applied in heart, conscience, and conduct. Such recognition and application was the work mostly of priests, psalmists, and wise men. These, although not always immediately gifted with a new or special insight into the nature of God and his dealings with them, yet lived in close contact with those who possessed primary inspiration. They thus could be described as possessing secondary inspiration. How high a degree depended on their relation to what was accepted as primary inspiration. Ecclesiastes, Chronicles, and Esther are books where the divine element is at a minimum. Books where the element is stronger are the Psalms, which cultivate and give expression to religious feeling, and the historical books, where inspiration lies not in the narration of events but in the interpretation of the divine purpose running through the history and the moral lessons drawn from a study of the past.

The most frustrating aspect of this account of inspiration is

The Inductive Approach 43

its elusiveness. When Sanday writes about the development of the biblical literature or summarizes the convictions that led to the formation of the canon, his work is a model of restrained, precise writing. When he begins to develop his theology of inspiration it is very difficult to determine what exactly he is claiming. Even when he pauses in his final chapter to summarize his position, one is still left with the feeling that the subject is as elusive as ever. On the whole Sanday concentrates more on telling us how to arrive at a proper account of inspiration than he does on actually developing a positive understanding of the matter. His basic thesis is that the prophets constitute the paradigm case for divine inspiration; it is they who show us what inspiration truly involves. But this of itself only takes us partially towards our goal, for we now want to know what they reveal as regards the nature of divine inspiration. Unfortunately Sanday for the most part wavers at this crucial point. One can read and re-read his lectures and still remain convinced that one has not laid hold of his theory of inspiration. One may be forgiven therefore if one is tempted to dismiss Sanday as hopelessly vague on the nature of inspiration.

For example, what is one to make of the following passage, where Sanday perhaps comes closest to a definition of inspiration? After pointing out that the Hebrew nation was chosen by God to be the recipients of the Bible he says this:

Just as one particular branch of one particular stock was chosen to be in a general sense the recipient of clearer revelation than was vouchsafed to others, so within that branch certain individuals were chosen to have their hearts and minds moved in a manner more penetrating and more effective than their fellows, with the result that their written words convey to us truths about the nature of God and His dealing with man which other writings do not convey with equal fulness, power, and purity. We say that this special moving is due to the action upon those hearts and minds of the Holy Spirit. And we call that action Inspiration.[7]

As it stands this passage leaves a lot to be desired. To be sure we are told what the result of inspiration is: it adds a special quality to the written words produced by an inspired individual. But this does not help much. At best we have the thesis that inspiration is some sort of action of the Holy

Spirit in the heart and mind of chosen persons in Israel. It would be difficult to improve on the vagueness of such a claim.

It is at this point that Sanday relies most heavily on the prophets to fill out his account of inspiration. Unfortunately what this in turn means is that unwittingly he is led to speak of inspiration in a way that perpetuates the confusing of divine inspiration with divine speaking. Thus when Sanday develops, albeit schematically, his account of the prophets, he invariably draws attention to their claim to be recipients of a special word from God. As we saw earlier it is their contention, in his view, that 'the thoughts which arose in their hearts and the words which arose to their lips were put there by God.'[8] Precisely the same movement of thought takes place when he discusses the inspiration of the apostles as revealed by Paul. In this case too the focus is on the apostle as a recipient of special revelation as Paul defends this in Galatians 1: 11-17. In other words what begins as a vague theory of inspiration develops under the influence of the biblical account of prophecy as a theory in which revelation and divine speaking increasingly occupy the centre of the stage. The net effect of this is that the whole idea of divine inspiration continues to be treated as if it were close to, if not identical with, divine revelation and divine speaking. This is no accident. So long as the prophets are treated as the paradigm of inspiration and so long as attention is concentrated on their claim to have received special revelation, then so long will divine speaking and divine dictating be in the background of the proposed analysis of inspiration. Obvious distinctions between the actions of speaking and inspiring become well-nigh forgotten. Sanday is no exception to this. Thus he can speak of the inspiration of the prophets at one stage as 'the gift by which God Himself *spake* through them and made them the channels of the communication of His will to men.' [my italics][9] And at times he can interchange the concepts of inspiration and revelation as if they were synonymous.[10]

It should come as no surprise, therefore, that Sanday is very reluctant to admit that he has departed in any radical manner from what he calls the traditional theory of

The Inductive Approach

inspiration. Once his own inductive theory is properly understood, 'the two theories will be found to approximate to each other more nearly, and even when they do not exactly meet the gap between them is in a manner bridged over.'[11] He continues elsewhere in the same vein: 'So far as they differ it would be rather in quantity, inasmuch as on the inductive view inspiration is not inherent in the Bible as such, but is present in different books and parts of books in different degrees.'[12] This avowal must be taken with the utmost seriousness. At heart Sanday is working with the central concepts of his own theological past. He is at one with that past in continuing to treat prophets as the paradigm case of divine inspiration. It is this that forms the link in his thinking between inspiration and revelation. Without this it is difficult to see why he should bring the two together in the first place.

Sanday is also at one with the past in relying heavily on the principle of extension to detect the presence of inspiration outside the prophetic material. The principle of extension was crucial to a thinker like Gaussen. Beginning with the prophets, Gaussen worked out from this centre to embrace the whole of the Bible as inspired by God. Sanday proceeds in the same direction but in his case inductive considerations enter in to give a crucial twist to the way in which the principle is applied.

In Gaussen's case the principle of extension led inevitably to a doctrine of inerrancy. Applying the prophetic claim to have received the word of God to the whole of the Bible, Gaussen argued that Scripture must be inerrant. As a consequence of this any critical procedure that clashed with this must be at fault. Sanday, however, gave logical priority at this point to the critical procedures. As a good historian he could not with integrity accept that the criticial procedures were mistaken. The way out of this difficulty was to interpret the principle of extension in a different manner from Gaussen. Rather than concentrate at this juncture on the form of the prophetic inspiration, Sanday concentrated on the content of the prophetic message. Inspiration in any particular writing was measured by discovering the degree to which that writing reflected the message of the prophets.

Thus he compared the revelation contained in the Old Testament to an inland lake which had several sources. Most of the water came from springs that penetrated deep down into the earth. However, 'the water which wells up from these hidden sources spreads out to meet the rills which come down from the surrounding slopes and absorbs them'.[13] In this analogy the hidden springs are the prophets and law-makers of Israel, i.e. the recipients of a direct commission from God. In so far as one had absorbed or been absorbed by the waters from these springs then so far was one inspired by God. Material outside the prophets might not be a main artery, but it could be a channel by which the purer waters of revelation were dispersed and brought to bear upon the life of men.

This approach to the principle of extension enabled Sanday to avoid a doctrine of inerrancy. It thus opened up space for him to apply his criticial skills to Scripture without sacrificing his commitment to inspiration. In fact he allows his findings on the critical level to have a bearing on decisions about the nature of inspiration as found in, say, the historical books of the Bible. The rôle such findings have, however, is entirely negative. The most that Sanday can report is that he can find no evidence that the inspiration of a historian 'in any way superseded the ordinary use of historical material, or that it interfered with that use in such a way as to prevent possibilities of error'.[14]

Taking Sanday's position as a whole we can say that it was a valiant attempt to bend traditional notions of inspiration to accommodate a criticial approach to Scripture. In method and in content Sanday failed to break sufficiently loose from the confusion of his predecessors. This judgement stands despite the suggestion of James Barr that Sanday was the key figure who persuaded the Anglican Church to abandon the theory of verbal inspiration.[15] If this is true it was more of a happy accident than a natural outcome. Sanday could have had this effect only if his theory was partially assimilated. This is a highly likely possibility in that his position does not form a coherent whole. Given the various strands operating in his thinking it is easy for the reader to latch on to one element and ignore the rest. Thus if one ignored his emphasis on the prophets but absorbed his general vagueness as expressed in claims about the action of the Holy Sprit, and at the same time agreed with his insistence that critical considerations be accepted, one could easily abandon a theory of verbal inspiration and yet still believe that one held a theory of inspiration derived from Sanday. What precisely such a theory would amount to is anyone's guess.

This is reflected in the fact that one rarely reads or hears of Sanday's theory of inspiration. Many know that he gave an important set of lectures on the topic but they find it difficult to summarize his positive contribution to the subject. One exception to this is R. P. C. Hanson who has suggested that Sanday's main point was that 'the Bible is inspired because it is inspiring'.[16] Sanday believed nothing of the kind. He rejected such a subjectivist understanding of inspiration. He believed in fact that inspiration was 'real and no fiction, a direct objective action of the Divine upon the Human'.[17] But as we have seen, it is far from clear what precise action he had in mind. In so far as he does fill in the details he falls back on the divine activity associated with the prophets, and thus perpetuates the assimilation of divine inspiration to divine speaking.

Writers in the inductive tradition as it has developed since Sanday's day seem to have ignored his contribution to the subject. However, they have tended to think along lines that are just about discernible in his lectures. To be sure, some have abandoned all hope of ever developing a doctrine of inspiration. Thus R. P. C. Hanson goes so far as to insist that the official doctrine on inspiration and the only plausible meaning to be attached to the concept is that provided by Origen. This view he outlines as follows:

> God was himself the author of holy Scripture and he dictated every word of it, though the writers did not actually lose consciousness as they were being inspired. The Bible therefore was inerrant, that is to say, accurate in every statement which it makes.[18]

Like Sanday he recognizes that one cannot hold this view and accept the results of historical criticism. But unlike Sanday he does not feel that the concept can be salvaged for today.

No alternative meaning of the word 'inspiration' when applied to the Bible has been produced which has any connection with the root meaning of the word itself or with Origen's definition of it. We still cling to the word, speaking of the Scripture but we can give no meaning to it which does not alter it into an entirely different concept unconnected with the traditional one. It would be much better to abandon the word altogether as a lingering vestige of the oracular view of the Bible and substitute another.[19]

Judging from the amount of space devoted to the idea of inspiration in current Systematic Theology one suspects that Hanson is not alone in his convictions about the matter. However, there are two lines of development that are worthy of mention. Each focuses on an element that occurs in Sanday. One focuses on the prophets as the paradigm case of inspiration. The other concentrates on the activity of the Holy Spirit as a clue to inspiration. Both presuppose, of course, that inductive considerations rule out any doctrine of inerrancy. Let us look at each of these in turn.

A view of inspiration that has surfaced frequently in the last hundred years is the view that the inspiration of the Bible is best understood as akin to aesthetic or intellectual inspiration. This position was held a generation ago by the influential Old Testament scholar H. Wheeler Robinson.[20] Robinson, who ended an illustrious career as Principal of Regent's Park College, Oxford, believed that there were striking resemblances between the inspiration of the ancient prophets and the inspiration of a great poet or scientist. All three were subject to an experience that integrated what he called compulsion and intuition. That is, they produced their best work not at will but as if borne along by a compelling force: this is the element of compulsion; and they often experienced a flash of discovery that completed a long process of thought on a particular subject: this is the element of intuition. In this experience all three brought forth in an articulate form some truth that already existed but as yet was not revealed to man. It was this that set them apart from others. What set the prophet apart in turn from the poet and scientist was the sphere in which he worked. The prophet's inspiration was exercised in the moral and religious sphere. Principally they were spokesmen for God. Because they

The Inductive Approach

were thus related to God their thought possessed a peculiar and intense note of authority. They were sent with the express purpose of getting something done; their emphasis was volitional. Also, because they worked in the religious sphere, they were especially dependent on intuition to evaluate what was precious rather than common in religious matters. This intuitional judgement was in turn exercised by those in later generations who responded to their message. There was a sense therefore in which Coleridge was right when he said that 'whatever *finds* me bears witness that it has proceeded from a Holy Spirit'.[21]

This account of inspiration has enormous appeal, especially to those who look at art or science as a means of establishing that theology has as much right to life as any other academic discipline. Within this framework religion and theology are supported by a theory of knowledge that attempts to bring together the genius of the great musician, artist, and scientist. Any such theory will be attractive to the modern religious mind, but especially to those who have themselves been trained as scientists and have developed a keen appreciation for the arts. Despite this I find this whole approach quite unsatisfactory.

First, this way of looking at inspiration invariably trades on an account of revelation that is open to question. Generally it asserts that God is revealing himself more or less to the same degree in all of history and creation. Unfortunately not everyone is aware of this. What is needed, therefore, is a highly sensitive religious mind that is sufficiently endowed with insight to bring to light what God is always and everywhere revealing himself. This need is met by the prophets, who, being inspired by God, somehow possess the required insight. Broadly speaking this is the general approach to revelation that lies behind the poetic theory of inspiration. No doubt it would need to be filled out in greater detail before receiving the full assessment it deserves. Here I simply want to register my radical dissent from its basic content. Putting the issue at its sharpest, this stance on revelation completely ignores the extent to which we are dependent on direct divine action to discern the mind and purpose of God. Consequently I am unimpressed by any account of inspiration that trades on such a weak concept of revelation.

Secondly – and here I merely broaden the matter – this vision of inspiration is in the end a modern attempt to salvage something of inspiration after all else has been surrendered to a naturalistic metaphysics. What this account seeks to do is to avoid at all cost any commitment to the idea of direct divine action in the world. Naturally in such a context it is comforting if one can believe that prophets can stand on the same footing as the great men of science, art, and literature. On the other hand, if one is not at all convinced of the truth of naturalism then the whole attempt to assimilate prophecy to poetry and the like is redundant. This is the way that I view the matter. In addition I am not at all sure that one can fit the phenomena of art, science, and religion into one overarching framework. At the very least this demands far more attention and thought than Robinson seems to have given to it. Given these misgivings, it is no surprise if one finds that the associated conception of inspiration is not very attractive. One simply wants to tackle the idea of inspiration from an entirely different perspective and thereby provide a different account of it.

Principally, one wishes to retain some element of objective divine activity. This seems to get lost in any view that would treat inspiration in the religious sense as parallel to inspiration in art or science. Those who stress the significance of poetic inspiration do not, of course, deny that God is at work in the lives of poets. But their conception of the divine action involved at this point is very general. On this view God is active in the work and lives of all great poets in the sense that he is the creative source and sustainer of all human life and activity. This dimension to divine activity is of enormous significance and it can all too easily be neglected or ignored. However it is questionable whether we should reduce divine inspirational activity to this very general level. I find it odd to speak of Mozart or Copernicus or Yeats as being divinely inspired. In fact we do not normally bring in the divine at all. We simply speak of them as being inspired or inspiring. I feel there is a clear distinction in meaning between being inspired or inspiring and being inspired by God. For me this distinction is to be located in the crucial role that is played by God's revelatory and relational activity in the lives of those he inspires. Just how this is to be developed will detain us in the next chapter. For the present it is sufficient to report that I consider it inappropriate to identify divine inspiration with ability to inspire. I see no reason to agree with Coleridge that 'whatever *finds* me bears witness for itself that it has proceeded from a Holy Spirit'. On the contrary I confess that much has found me that I would judge to be proceeding from anywhere or anybody but a Holy Spirit. The mere fact that it finds me is a hopelessly inadequate criterion for discerning divine inspiration, for it opens the door to all sorts of dangerous nonsense dressed out in the garments of inspiration. In any case this whole perspective on inspiration does little to throw any light on what inspiration is in itself.

The position just described focuses on the prophets as the crucial starting-point for a true understanding of inspiration. We can detect here at least an affinity with the outlook of Sanday. A position which also shares an affinity with Sanday has been developed by an Oxford scholar of a later generation, namely James Barr, who is presently Professor of Hebrew. Barr concentrates on the action of the Holy Spirit as the clue to inspiration. We saw that this element in Sanday's work was weak in that it was very vague. It will be of interest to see if Barr can avoid this defect in his account.

James Barr is not a theologian whom one would automatically associate with a positive account of inspiration. He is more widely known as a penetrating critic of much traditional thinking on the subject. In his recent book, *Fundamentalism,*[22] he launched a major assault on recent Evangelical thinking on inspiration and related convictions. Before that he wrote extensively in the general area of biblical studies, offering a devastating critique of much modern thinking about the Bible and its interpretation.[23] All that he has written in this field is exceptionally incisive, illuminating, and rewarding. Behind it lies an obvious concern to abolish shabby and unfounded notions of the Bible and our study of it. There also lies behind it a very definite concern to see Scripture enrich our present situation in the Church.

> ... I believe that many of the troubles of modern Christianity are self-inflicted burdens which would be lightened if the message of the Bible were more highly regarded. I have no faith in the vision of a Christianity which would emancipate itself more completely from biblical influence and go forward bravely, rejoicing in its own contemporary modernity. On the contrary, if there are resources for the liberation of the churches and their message, these resources lie to a considerable degree within the Bible.[24]

It is easy to miss this concern in Barr's work. But it is certainly there and it is clearly reflected in his attempt to provide a positive account of the status of the Bible in the Christian faith. For obvious reasons our exposition focuses on what he has to say about inspiration.

To some extent Barr is uncertain whether the term 'inspiration' can be revitalized for use today. He is in the end convinced, however, that it stands for something that is essential in a Christian account of the status of the Bible.

> It expresses the belief . . . that in some way the Bible comes from God, that he has in some sense a part in its origin, that there is a linkage between the basic mode through which he has communicated with man and the coming into existence of this body of literature.[25]

This very general comment on inspiration is obviously vague. Barr is fully aware of this. As he himself points out the phrase 'in some way' highlights the problem, for 'we do not have any idea of ways in which God might straightforwardly communicate articulate thoughts or sentences to men . . .'[26] Traditional thinking is unhelpful to Barr at this point, so there is no use in envisaging a special mode of direct communication from God to persons like prophets. So where do we turn? He answers as follows:

> Today, I think we believe, or have to believe that God's communication with the men of the biblical period was not any different from the mode of his communication with his people today. 'Inspiration' would then mean that the God whom we worship was also likewise in contact with his people in ancient times, and that in their particular circumstances, in the stage in which they existed, he was present in the formation of their tradition and in the crystallization of that tradition as Scripture; but that the mode of this contact was not different from the mode in which God has continued to to make himself known to men.[27]

The Inductive Approach 53

As they stand, these further developments are also rather vague. Barr is candid enough to admit this. Discussing the question of the mode in which God is with his people and thus inspiring their tradition, he says:

> I confess I do not understand this well, but two thoughts may be offered to readers. First, 'the Spirit' in contexts of this kind seems to be used for a sort of linkage of meaning with presence. When human words about God are spoken, they have to be heard 'in the Spirit' in order to be rightly understood; not because the Spirit furnishes the intellectual links but because when the words are understood they are accompanied by a mode of presence of the one of whom they speak. If this can be said of the understanding of scripture, it can perhaps be said also of the process of production of that same scripture. The relation of the biblical writers and traditionists to God through the Spirit is thus not basically other than that of the church today in its listening to God. There is however a difference in the *stage* at which things are: the biblical men had a pioneering role in the formulation of our classic model, and this may make it fitting for them to be called 'inspired' in a special sense. The second point is this: in this exposition I have tried to avoid what is called a 'God-of-the-gaps' strategy, that is, an approach which explains everything possible on a human, historical and scientific level but then, at such points as show gaps in explanation at that level, suddenly ascribes the filling of the gap to the agency of God. If I understand rightly, the idea of the Spirit is of one who *accompanies* human thought and action; the human thought and action, however, can be given human and historical description, without resort to supernatural interventions at any points of difficulty. In giving an account of the nature of the Bible, this aspect appeals to me.[28]

This amplifies his meaning considerably. He is now suggesting that the relation between the Holy Spirit and the people of God was the same yesterday as it is today, and that to speak of 'inspiration' is to speak of the relationship between the Spirit and the people of God. Christians experience the work of the Spirit in their response to God in the present. The divine Spirit presently indwells Christians, confirming the reality of God's salvation and providing the sustenance for Christian living. They are inspired by the Spirit of God. Likewise God's people of old were inspired by the Spirit and out of their relationship with the Spirit they gradually developed traditions which became in time Scripture.[29]

This analysis of inspiration is of obvious interest. It will be particularly attractive to those who feel that inspiration has not ceased with the closing of the canon. The emphasis on present inspiration is enough to satisfy in this respect. It will likewise be appealing to those who are uneasy with or hostile to any commitment to direct divine action in the world. Barr speaks for many when he eschews any resort to supernatural intervention. He does, of course, qualify his hostility, for he is only opposed to the resort to divine intervention at any point of difficulty. But given that most opposed to supernatural intervention oppose it because they feel it always involves a 'God-of-the-gaps' theology and thus always involves difficulty, this qualification does not count for much.

The fundamental problem with Barr's proposal is that it is still much too vague and obscure. The key point is this: Barr has not told us enough about God's present mode of contact with his people for us to be clear about the past mode of contact. The analogy between present and past could be helpful but as it stands it is empty. So long as this remains, the associated idea of inspiration remains hidden from view. All we know is that present and past are the same as regards God's mode of contact with his people.

The general framework of Barr's ideas may well explain why his position is inevitably vague. When one examines his position carefully, one discovers that he is still working within the general area staked out for inspiration by writers like Gaussen and Warfield. It is difficult to establish this conclusively, but it seems likely to be true. Gaussen and those who followed his lead confused divine inspiration with divine speaking. More generally they failed to keep divine inspiration sufficiently apart from divine revelation. Thus the Bible was for them the locus of special revelation because it was regarded as having been given word for word by God. The Bible was spoken by God; what the Bible says God says; hence it is special revelation. Barr, although appreciative of the significance of divine speaking within the biblical traditions, has difficulty in making sense of it in modern terms. He has equal difficulty in appropriating the concept of revelation. Thus far has Barr broken with the classical Christian tradition. However, he has still remained within this whole area by retaining an interest in and

The Inductive Approach 55

emphasis on divine communication. Barr refuses to speak of revelation but he does use a term that is related to revelation when he prefers to stress the less loaded term 'communication'. Thus he is happy to write of 'God's communication with the men of the biblical period'. This he tells us is not any different from 'the mode of his communication with his people today.'[30] It is this notion that is the starting-point for his analysis of inspiration. Indeed his proposals about inspiration are intimately related to his convictions about the nature and meaning of all divine communication. But having rejected the classical ingredients of special revelation, all that he has left to fall back on are rather general remarks about the work of the Holy Spirit in the life of God's people. This whole area is itself beset with confusion at present, so it is not surprising that Barr is at a loss how to articulate what is involved. All this in turn finds its way back into his account of inspiration, for he has to rely on the one to explain the other.

Barr might protest that these comments, as much as my basic objection to his position, assume a confidence in our ability to articulate the meaning of inspiration and thus to provide a clearer account of it than he has furnished. This confidence, he may say, is unjustified. My understanding of his position is that he considers the concept of inspiration to be an extrapolation from other religious concepts that apply to God in a more or less direct manner.[31] In his view, therefore, a true analysis of inspiration will seem vague, for it will be at least one remove from the primary concepts we apply to God.

Barr may well be correct in this, but I am not convinced that he is. He surely owes it to us to clarify and defend the underlying account of religious language on which his theory of inspiration rests. Until such time as he does this his position remains obscure. In the meantime we should not become too pessimistic about the degree of clarity that is possible in our vision of divine inspiration. At the very least we should bend our efforts to attain as much clarity as possible before we give up in despair.

It is precisely this whole dimension that is missing in the writings of those committed to an inductive approach to inspiration. They have failed to articulate their account of the meaning of religious discourse. They are so intent on avoiding an account of inspiration that might seem to question the phenomena of the Bible that they do not pay sufficient attention to the conceptual dimension of the issue. To be sure, there is advantage in insisting that inductive considerations be taken seriously. The chief and enduring merit of the inductive approach is its insistence that a responsible doctrine of inspiration must reckon with the Bible as we have it. Perhaps the major break-through at this point was made by Sanday, although this is of little importance. What really matters is that we recognize that the production of the Bible was a complex, dynamic affair. We must also recognize the existence of mistakes of one sort or another. In other words our doctrine of Scripture must rest in part on inductive considerations. It must take account of what is known of Scripture when it is examined by the canons of evidence that we rely on generally in our everyday lives. Otherwise we are living in a world of theological fantasy manufactured out of a conceptual analysis that is unrelated to the world we inhabit.

Barr, Robinson, and Sanday are weak in their analysis of the concept of inspiration – what we mean when we say that the Bible is inspired by God. In part this is due to their concentration on purely inductive considerations. By nature and training Barr, Robinson, and Sanday are first and foremost historians and linguists, although they can ably range outside this specialist trade in their work. But what we need is a complement to this work. We need to pursue in its own right an analysis of the concept of inspiration.

Strange as it may seem, I think that Warfield came close to recognizing this need. In a remark on 2 Tim. 3: 16, he pointed out that inspiration calls for an investigation not of what the Scriptures are but of what Paul means by the term 'inspiration'.[32] To my mind these are not mutually exclusive. After all, in the context Paul is referring to an existing body of literature, and we must allow the nature of that literature to have some bearing on what Paul means by inspiration. Otherwise our exegesis is unhistorical and unreal. On the other hand Warfield is correct to insist that this alone is insufficient. It is not enough to give a description of the Bible as we have it, ascribing to it say qualities x, y, and z, and then simply insist that these qualities explain what is meant by inspiration. This is too simplistic. There is surely more to divine inspiration than this if the concept is to have any substantial content.

At this juncture Warfield insisted that what was needed was exegetical study of the word 'inspiration' and an inductive study of what the Bible teaches about inspiration. This is a sound observation. There are indeed exegetical and biblical considerations that require attention and we shall come to these later. But what Warfield fails to recognize is that there is also a conceptual dimension of our theme that is logically distinct from both exegesis and biblical theology. We need to analyse the verb 'inspire' as predicated of God, to compare and contrast it with other divine activity, to draw out its implications and map its relations to other key concepts and categories. What is required is sensitive conceptual analysis. Such a study must draw on general considerations about the nature of religious language to indicate how divine activity like inspiration should be understood. In broad terms it is an effort to clarify the logic of the term 'inspire' as predicated of God. To that we now turn.

3

THE CONCEPT OF INSPIRATION

IF there is one mistake in recent theories of inspiration which deserves to be singled out for special attention, that mistake is at root conceptual. Rather than pause to reflect on divine inspiration, Evangelical theologians have built their theories around the idea of divine speaking. This is simply a basic category mistake. It is essential to identify and remove this mistake if there is to be progress or hope for any future account of inspiration. Virtually all the theories that we have examined are defective at this point. Indeed so widespread and all-pervasive is the conceptual confusion here that I have some sympathy with those who feel that it is impossible to rebuild or repair the concept for today. However, once my main point is grasped there can be a radical shift of vision that is liberating and refreshing to those who can accept it. Let me approach the matter from a general angle.

The fundamental conception of God that informs the Christian tradition is that God is a transcendent, personal agent. As some recent theologians have insisted, God is first and foremost the one who acts. But this very general account of who God is must be filled out by specifying more exactly what God has actually done. Otherwise all we have is a general, if not abstract, concept that fails to relate God to the world of both everyday life and religious experience. Christians have not hesitated to execute this task, although they have always recognized that this generates sophisticated and specialist philosophical and theological discussion. Thus Christians have said that God created the world *ex nihilo* and that he continues to sustain it by his power. God liberated the Hebrew slaves from Egypt and he spoke to the people of Israel and Judah through the prophets. God became incarnate in history in Jesus of Nazareth. He

The Concept of Inspiration

performed miracles; for example, he raised Jesus from the dead. He sent the Holy Spirit to the waiting disciples on the day of Pentecost and guided the early missionary efforts of the Church. And so one could continue to list the various acts and activities that God has done and one could add to that list by specifying what God continues to do and what he will do in the future. Without the fundamental category of agency we have ceased to be theists, for theism by definition is belief in a personal God who is analogous in crucial respects to human agents. Without some specification of what God has done and is doing we would be left with a very general concept that would be too far removed from life and experience to be religiously satisfying. We fill out and elaborate our fundamental picture of God by spelling out in detail what God has done, is doing, and will do.

As one might expect, philosophers and theologians have been puzzled by the idea of a divine agent. This is not surprising, for it is part of their job to examine such concepts as agency, event, revelation, persons, causation, etc. Sometimes they have been interested in the particular acts attributed to God by Christians. Thus the miraculous acts of God have for centuries been a source of analysis and controversy. In more recent days fundamental questions have been raised by the very idea of a divine agent, although these questions are not entirely new. Thus theologians have turned to other categories such as 'being' and 'process' instead of agency as a means of understanding God. Philosophers, on the other hand, have seriously wondered whether the idea of an incorporeal agent is coherent or not. To many philosophers the idea of a body is constitutive of the concept of an agent, so to talk of a divine agent is sheer nonsense, for God by definition does not have a body. For my part I am entirely happy with the idea of God as an agent. I find no insuperable logical dificulties in this notion and I see no need to substitute other fundamental categories for it. Moreover I find no insurmountable philosophical problems in assenting to such a miracle as the resurrection. Indeed I find traditional Christian thinking both religiously and intellectually enriching and exciting in both these areas. That God is a bodiless agent and that he has performed miracles in the past pose no insuperable conceptual, historical or religious difficulties for me; on the contrary they are central to my whole conception and experience of God.

What has been more of a puzzle to me is how we are to construe those predicates that ascribe particular actions to God. For example, how are we to understand the claim that God spoke to the prophets? It is far from easy to determine how exactly we are to explain the logic of such expressions as 'God spoke to Moses on Mount Sinai' or 'God spoke to Paul on the road to Damascus'. Within this enquiry there are two distinct questions. On the one hand we need to know what function these expressions are intended to have. Are they splendid poetry or factual prose? Are they intended to induce religious feelings of a special kind or to report an ineffable religious experience or to inform us of certain significant religious facts? Let us for the moment suppose that their function is primarily informative rather than, say, emotive. Let us say that they are intended as serious factual discourse, and in so doing let us leave aside the delicate and difficult matter of why this is so. For the moment let us simply accept that this is a plausible answer to our query. Having gone thus far we notice that we have a further question to answer: how are we to interpret 'speaking' when predicated of God? Are we to imagine that God spoke in an audible voice, in a fashion very similar to human speaking? Or are we to think of the speech of God as something unique and interior, something that involved an inner voice but no outer noises, say, rather like a form of telepathy? Whatever our answer to this question we can readily identify it as being logically quite distinct from the first one mentioned above.

Recent philosophical theology has been much concerned with questions of this kind. This concern is legitimate and absorbing. Such questions about the meaning of religious discourse are the most important posed by religion in our day. They are inescapable for the contemporary theologian, and how we answer them will determine the whole foundation and structure of our thinking about God. For the most part our concentration has focused on the first kind of question I identified. Since the challenge of logical Positivism in the 1930s much effort has been spent on clarifying the logic of religious discourse but to date there is no agreement in the answers given. My own view is quite simple: much fundamental religious language is intended to inform us about the way things are, and it succeeds in this respect.[1]

However, we also need to attend to the second sort of question identified. We need to clarify how we are to understand the verbs that attribute certain specific actions or activities to God. The traditional answer has involved a doctrine of analogy. When we use the verb 'speak' for example, in relation to God, it does not carry all the meaning that it has in everyday discourse when it is used of human agents, but only some of it. 'Speak' as predicated of God is neither univocal or equivocal; it is analogous to 'speak' as predicated of human agents. As I see it, some doctrine of analogy is indispensable in any coherent account of the meaning of religious language. Without it we slide into either empty equivocation or radical agnosticism in our thinking about God. But our doctrine must be less formal and mathematical than that traditionally developed by Aquinas and his followers. That is, we have to rely on sensitive conceptual judgement in determining how analogous language is to operate. There is an irreducible element of mystery and personal linguistic judgement in our use of religious discourse for which we need make no apology. This position has been expounded with characteristic grace by Basil Mitchell. In general terms he puts it in this way:

> . . . a word should be presumed to carry with it as many of the original entailments as the new context allows, and this is determined by the other descriptions which there is reason to believe also apply to God. That God is incorporeal dictates that 'father' does not mean 'physical progenitor', but the word continues to bear the connotation of tender protective care. Similarly God's 'wisdom' is qualified by the totality of other descriptions which are applicable to him; it does not, for example, have to be learned, since he is omniscient and eternal.[2]

This general proposal has crucial implications about our understanding of discourse about divine inspiration. It entails that we must first consider the word 'inspire' as it applies to human agents, if we are ever to understand it as applied to God. It is precisely this that the theologians we examined earlier failed to do. They made two fatal mistakes. first of all they ignored the need to begin with human agents; instead they began, continued, and ended with God. Secondly, they failed to focus on inspiration; they focused instead on speaking. As a result the whole character of divine inspiration was misread from the outset. They failed to attend to the root meaning of the word 'inspire' and failed in turn to exercise sensitive conceptual judgement in applying it to God. To grasp this point is to lay hold of one of the pivotal considerations that led me to develop a revised account of inspiration.

To avoid any misunderstanding here let me hasten to insist that this is a fundamental procedural consideration that demands attention in its own right. I am not at this point engaging in exegesis; this will come later. Nor am I suggesting that we reduce divine inspiration to human inspiration, for this is an absurdity that ignores the need to specify how divine inspiration differs from human inspiration, and I will do this shortly. My contention concerns the logic of the term 'inspire' as applied to God. In the case of other words we instinctively employ the procedure I am advocating. When we say that God loves us or that God knows that London is the capital of England or that God forgives us our sins, we grasp what these expressions mean by unconsciously drawing on the meaning that the terms 'love', 'know', 'forgive' possess in everyday language when applied to human agents. In the case of 'inspire' it is precisely this that we have failed to do. Instead we have focused on divine speaking, and even then we have failed to specify, if only in broad terms, how such speaking is to be related or compared to those human situations in which we first learn the meaning of our language. We need to retrace our steps and re-examine the concept of divine inspiration in the light of the principles we follow in other cases of divine action.

The term 'inspire' as developed theologically derives from its use in 2 Tim. 3: 16. The Greek word here is θεόπνευστος, which literally means 'God-breathed'. Virtually all translations express the sense of this by means of the phrase 'inspired by God'. This is entirely correct in that it is in keeping with the etymology of the English verb 'inspire', which is, in fact, derived from the Latin verb *spirare*, 'to breathe'. Our English verb 'inspire' therefore supplies quite neatly what is required by the Greek. Indeed Sanday points out that 2 Tim. 3: 16 is the only passage 'in which a direct equivalent for our word "inspired" occurs in the Bible.'[3]

This insight provides the clue to the first stage of a proper account of divine inspiration. Divine inspiration, I suggest, must be rooted in an adequate conception of what it is for one agent to inspire another. In other words, we must concentrate on the meaning of 'inspire' as used in everyday contexts before we turn to what it means as applied to God. By so doing we shall be attending to the root meaning of the concept.

The best way to begin this is to look closely at a paradigm case of inspiration as it operates in the common world of human agents. Out of this we can specify some important and necessary features of the meaning of the term 'inspire'. That done, we need to declare how the term is to be qualified when it is applied to God. Beyond this we can pause to answer some objections to our positive proposals about divine inspiration.

Our choice of a paradigm case of inspiration is always a delicate affair. There is no rigid set of procedures to determine our decisions at this level. We need to be sensitive and look for an example that will be illuminating rather than one that will be perfect in some absolute sense. A familiar case that I find helpful is furnished by a good teacher inspiring his students. Imagine for a moment a situation where we would naturally say that a teacher had inspired his students. Think of the light that this throws on the meaning of inspiration. We should note the following features as being essential to the description of the process.

First, since the students will vary in ability, temperament, and interests, and since the intensity of their relationship may also vary, it is perfectly in order to speak of degrees of inspiration. There is no guarantee that inspiration will be uniform, flat, or uneven in its effects. Indeed it should surprise us if it were so. Secondly, there is no question of the students remaining passive while they are being inspired. On the contrary: their natural abilities will be used to the full and as a result they will show great differences in style, content, and vocabulary. Their native intelligence and talent will be greatly enhanced and enriched but in no way obliterated or passed over. Thirdly, as there will be other influences and sources of inspiration at work upon them, there need be no surprise if, from the point of view of the teacher, they make mistakes. Commonly students in acknowledging the assistance and inspiration of their teachers dissociate them from any mistakes they may have made.

On the actual activity of inspiring there are two interesting points to be made. First, inspiring is not something that is done independently of other acts performed by the teacher. 'Inspiring', that is, is a polymorphous concept. It is not something that an agent does independently of other specifiable activity. One inspires someone in, with, and through other acts that one performs. Compare at this juncture another polymorphous concept – farming. One farms by ploughing fields, driving tractors, milking cows, tending sheep, going to market, etc. Farming is not something one does over and above such activity; it is done through them. Similarly with inspiring. A good teacher inspires through his supervision, teaching, lecturing, discussing, publishing, etc. He does not inspire independently of such activity. As a result – and here we arrive at the second point – the actual inspiring will generally be quite unconscious and unintentional on the part of the teacher. He may be quite unaware that his activity has this extra dimension to it, and that his students are being inspired by his routine work and example.

Finally we can note certain points about the effects of inspiration in the work produced by the students. To begin with, there are no hard and fast rules for detecting such effects. Normally we are persuaded by several strands of evidence taken together. The testimony of the students themselves will usually count for a lot. But there will probably be other considerations like continuity of interests, outlook, and perhaps even style of approach to the issue in hand. As to the actual content of the inspired work, we can make two comments with a reasonable degree of assurance. Where several people are inspired by the same agent, there will be some degree of unity in it, although how much will be difficult to specify in advance. Secondly, there will not be too radical a divergence from the views of the teacher, although again there can be no predictions in advance.

Given this description of a paradigm case of inspiration we can summarize the key features of the concept. I suggest that there are at least two that are constitutive. First, inspiration is a unique, irreducible activity that takes place between personal agents, one of whom, the inspirer, makes a definite objective difference to the work of the other, the inspired, without obliterating or rendering redundant the native activity of the other. Secondly, inspiration is a polymorphous concept in that it is achieved in, with, and through other acts that an agent performs. Both these features are surely minimal requirements in any analysis of inspiration. Therefore when we talk of the inspiration of God both these elements must be preserved. Without them the connections with the non-theological employment of the word have been so whittled away that one says nothing at all about God. With them the term is given substantial content.

The next task is a delicate and difficult one. We need to outline how far the other features identified can be presumed to apply when the term is used of God in his relation to those who gave us the Bible. In other words we must determine how far the term has to be qualified when it is predicated of God.

Very generally we should note immediately that the analogy has its limitations. the analogy between teacher and student is a highly intellectualist analogy. There is some virtue in this, for the divine inspiration of the Bible has traditionally been associated with instruction and teaching. The Bible certainly does have this rôle and deserves to have it. However, the analogy has its limits and short-comings. It is heavily cerebral in its connotations. More particularly it does not do adequate justice to the diversity and cruciality of the acts through which God has inspired the writers of the Bible. I propose that we correct this by noting that God principally but not exclusively inspired the writers of the Bible in, with, and through that sequence of his actions which reveals his heart and mind and saves us from our sins. Let me explain what I mean.

As we noted earlier, for Christians God is essentially a transcendent agent who has acted decisively in the world to reveal his intentions and purposes for that world and to redeem it from spiritual corruption. These special acts of God are not his only acts. He is doing and has done many other things. For example, at this very moment God sustains me as I write this sentence. If he did not do this I could not, on a Christian understanding of the world, continue to exist, nor to speak, nor think and write as I do. Yet no one would seriously suggest that this activity of God reveals anything significant about the intentions or purposes of God. The same can be said of many human activities. There is nothing necessarily or especially revealing, for example, in my scratching my ear or blowing my nose. Within the total set of acts and activity that an agent performs some are picked out as revelatory while others are not. Why and on what basis need not detain us here. All we need note is that the principle applies to both human agents and to God.

Traditionally Christians have proclaimed that there are two *loci* for God's revelatory acts, or for revelation. There is first the general revelation that God makes of his power and intelligence in creation as a whole. Through the general order, diversity, and brilliance of the created world God reveals his power and wisdom. In addition to this, however, he has intervened in the world in acts of special revelation. These acts fall into three classes. There are the acts of God in the history of Israel, especially his delivery of the Hebrew slaves from bondage in Egypt. Then there are the speech-acts of God in which he reveals his saving intentions and purposes to chosen prophets and apostles. Finally there are his unique and climactic acts in the life, death, and resurrection of Jesus of Nazareth. These latter acts of God constitute special revelation. As such they are at the heart of the Christian faith as it has been traditionally understood. Moreover they serve to distinguish the Christian faith from other faiths such as Deism, Judaism, or Islam.

Let it be emphasized again that these are not the only acts that God performs. God still speaks and comforts, he works in history, he brings people to new life, he forgives prodigals their sins, he promises the humble eternal life, he meets the meek in worship and in nature, he guides and directs his pilgrim people, etc. But such claims as these are made against a background wherein it is agreed that God has revealed himself uniquely in certain acts in the past and these acts serve as a criterion of what is to count as his acts today. What I am suggesting with respect to inspiration is simply this. It is through his revelatory and saving acts as well as through his personal dealings with individuals and groups that God inspired his people to write and collate what we now know as the Bible. Inspiration is not an activity that should be experientially separated from these other acts that God has performed in the past. As a matter of logic, inspiration is a unique activity of God that cannot be defined in terms of his other acts or activity, but as a matter of fact he inspires in, with, and through his special revelatory acts and through his personal guidance of those who wrote and put together the various parts of the Bible. This is the heart of my positive proposal.

In what other ways should our original analogy be qualified? Perhaps there are two. First, because God is omniscient he will be aware that he is inspiring in a way that human agents are not, therefore inspiration on his part will be fully intentional. God knows the nature and consequences of his acts in a way and to a degree that transcends human knowing, so all that he does is done intentionally rather than accidentally or without his knowledge. Secondly, because God is not an agent who can be located in the world of space and time, claims about the operation of his inspiration will be difficult to justify. We cannot, for example, show that God is active in the life of individuals or groups and thus is inspiring them with the same degree of ease as we do with human examples. This is not to say that we should be sceptical or diffident about claims to divine inspiration. It simply means that the process of justification must of necessity be more complex and indirect. Nor should this in itself surprise us, for the justification of claims about any divine action or activity is widely recognized to be far more complex and difficult than claims about human action or activity. And we all know how difficult the latter can be at times.

Beyond these qualifications I see no reason why the other features of inspiration identified should not be retained when we speak of the divine inspiration of the Bible. Some may need to be restated in a different way but this is a matter that need not detain us unduly. We can summarize the main points this way. When we speak of the divine inspiration of the Bible it is legitiate to talk in terms of degrees of inspiration; to insist on the full, indeed heightened, use of native ability in the creation of style, content, vocabulary etc.; to note that there is no guarantee of inerrancy, since agents, even when inspired by God, can make mistakes; and finally to infer that inspiration will result, first, in some kind of unity within the biblical literature and secondly in the committal to writing of a reliable and trustworthy account of God's revelatory and saving acts for mankind.

Perhaps a brief explanation of this last point is needed. It may well be wondered why it should be said that inspiration will result in a reliable account of God's saving acts. The answer is very simple. It stems from God's unique status as the agent of inspiration in question. With human agents there can be no guarantee that the content of what they inspire will be reliable or trustworthy, for human agents are by nature fallible and therefore quite as liable to inspire falsehood as truth It is very different with God, for he by definition, is omniscient and infallible. Therefore what he inspires will bear significant marks of truth and reliability. When this is added to what Christians maintain about the acts of God in the past, this has obvious consequences for the content of the Bible as inspired by God. This point was well made by John Baillie in a comment he made some years ago on the Bible as a witness to those events that constitute revelation.

. . . we cannot believe that God, having performed His mighty acts and having illumined the minds of prophet and apostle to understand their true import, left the prophetic and apostolic testimony to take care of itself. It were indeed a strange conception of the divine providential activity which would deny that the biblical writers were divinely assisted in their attempt to communicate to the world the illumination which, for the worlds sake, they had themselves received. The same Holy Spirit who had enlightened them into their own salvation must also have aided their efforts, whether spoken or written, to convey the message of salvation to those whom their words would reach.[4]

One has only to reflect on the foregoing analysis of inspiration to recognize how far removed divine inspiration is from divine speaking. The two are related, of course. It is partly through speaking to various significant individuals that God inspires them and others to write, edit, collate and preserve the various traditions that go to make up the Bible. But the relation between speaking and inspiration is contingent; there is no necessity for divine inspiration to be accomplished through divine speaking. Thus the relation cannot be one of identity, as so much writing on inspiration either states or presumes.

Once one grasps the full content of this analysis of inspiration it is a liberating experience, especially for anyone reared on the standard orthodoxy of the last generation. For a start, this account is compatible with what is generally known about the origin and character of the biblical writings. It lacks the artificiality that was prevalent in previous views. It is genuinely at home with differences in style and viewpoint, with differences of emphasis and vocabulary and with the existence of borderline books in the canon, i.e. books that were almost excluded from the Bible. It also allows a substantial role for critical historical investigation. Not only do we need sensitive historical judgement to engage in exegesis and the understanding of the various genres of literature to be found in Scripture, we also need it to fill out the degree to which this or that part of the Bible can be said to be historically reliable. Within the general framework sketched there is room for diversity of opinion on this or that part of the biblical tradition. We cannot tell in advance what parts are reliable and to what degree; historical study will have a genuine role to play in our assurance about reliability. For example, it is an open question whether Jonah was an historical figure or not; it is an open question how far the Pentateuch derives from Moses; it is an open question as to how far the Gospel of John is chronologically accurate. Such matters as these cannot be decided in advance. We must allow a genuine freedom to God as he inspires his chosen witnesses, knowing that what he does will be adequate for his saving and sanctifying purposes for our lives. In so doing we escape the tension and artificiality of those theories that have staked everything on the perfectionist and utopian hopes that stem from a theology of Scripture that substitutes divine speaking for divine inspiration without biblical or rational warrant.

Many Evangelicals are reluctant to recognize the need to acknowledge openly and explicitly that this evaluative process is entirely legitimate. To be sure, as I argued earlier, it is difficult to avoid engaging in such evaluation, for history is too important and indispensable a subject to be ignored today. As a matter of actual fact therefore Evangelicals have gone along with this process and some have even sought in a determined, if not exaggerated manner, to make apologetic advantage out of this necessity. However, this evaluative process has had strict limits built into it from the outset in that under no circumstances was it allowed that true, critical evaluation of the Bible had discovered any errors or mistakes. At this point the commitment either to dictation or to acts of God that are in substance identical with dictation reveals itself with a vengeance. Consider it this way.

Evangelicals tend at times to picture the evaluative process as the purely negative one of finding mistakes. A frantic panic can set in as they conjure up the image of the Christian scholar going through his Bible destructively striking this verse and that verse from the canon. Added to this is the conviction that the critical process must be subjective in the worst sense of that term. This in turn generates the fear that there will be no end to the process. If this verse is mistaken in the slightest degree then who is to assure us that the whole lot is not mistaken. The proverbial camel, we are told, will not be content merely to put his nose into the tent, he will insist on taking over the whole tent and thus raising it to the winds.

We are all familiar with this outlook and it helps to explain the genuine attraction that inerrancy can have for both scholar and student. As such it deserves to be treated with both pastoral sensitivity and with intellectual sympathy. But it must not be allowed to coerce us theologically into an inadequate analysis of inspiration. Not only does such an outlook forget that the critical process is positively enriching and illuminating, for it has brought countless riches to our faith and understanding. Not only does it trade on a massive failure of nerve which overlooks the fact that the canons of evaluation are not viciously subjective. Not only does it ignore the fact that we gladly engage in such evaluation every time we read a newspaper, listen to a conversation, or study a learned article. Principally such an attitude trades on a theory of divine dictation. Why is the historian not allowed to find mistakes in the Bible? Because on this view every word of the Bible has been given by God. God being omniscient and infallible obviously does not make mistakes, therefore it is impertinent if not blasphemous for anyone, be he scholar or not, to challenge the word of God. The logic is impeccable but the minor premise of the argument is mistaken. It has never been shown that God spoke or dictated every word of the Bible. This is a hangover from writers like Gaussen and others who had simply failed to distinguish inspiration from speaking or dictation. This pervasive confusion continues to surface when we examine the central objections that are liable to be made against my proposal. Before we look at these, let me make an additional point about inspiration.

The account of inspiration developed above allows us to make use of this term outside the confines of the writing and production of the Bible. Many Christians have felt it odd to suppose that inspiration should have suddenly dried up and stopped with the closing of the canon; as if God suddenly called a halt to his inspiring activity. In this they are surely correct. Our analysis of inspiration can accommodate this insight without strain or artificiality. Given what I have suggested about inspiration we can see how it applies to various situations. We can talk of the ordinary Christian who is coping heroically with the burdens of life as being inspired by God. We can say the same for the faithful preacher and pastor persistently building up the people of God in the faith, for the extraordinary saint giving up all in self-sacrifice for the poor and the needy, and for the persuasive evangelist proclaiming the good news of the Gospel to the outsider. I see no reason why we cannot today be inspired by God just as people of old were inspired by God. By exposure to his saving and revelatory acts in the past, by radical openness to the work of the Holy Spirit, and by diligent, sincere, and regular use of the classical means of grace, God will inspire us in the present to proclaim the Gospel, to live out its demands in the world, and think out its implications for our understanding of the issues and problems of our day and generation. In all these cases talk of divine inspiration is entirely appropriate; it is intellectually satisfying and spiritually liberating. Through his mighty acts of the past and through his continued activity in the present God continues to inspire his people.

It is at this point that many contemporary Evangelicals will be tempted to call an abrupt halt to my proposals. Were it not radical enough to suggest that inspiration does not guarantee total historical reliability, it will certainly be felt that the extending of inspiration to cover the lives of ordinary Christians is far beyond the bounds of acceptability. By this point, it might be said, the term has become so stretched and diluted as to be unworthy of significant use.

I have great sympathy with those who would raise this kind of objection. I can only hope that they will pause and ask themselves why exactly they feel this way. Their objection should not trouble us unduly. On the contrary we should be concerned if it was not raised with some force. I see in it, in fact, a reassertion of the view that divine inspiration is to be understood primarily in terms of divine speaking and divine revelation. For why do people feel uneasy about seeing inspiration at work today? The main reason is that they associate divine inspiration exclusively with the Bible. It is inspiration that safeguards for them the uniqueness and authority of the Bible. If we ask further why the Bible is inspired, we shall be told it is because it embodies God's true word to the world. But this simply confuses revelation and inspiration. It is one thing to say that the Bible contains God's special revelation to mankind and that it is the record of God's saving and revelatory acts and therefore authoritative for faith and practice. This is quite correct, as I see it. It is another thing entirely to say that the

The Concept of Inspiration

Bible was written and produced under divine inspiration. It is only because the two are confused that people are reluctant to recognize genuine cases of divine inspiration outside the Bible.

Mark carefully that in the objection considered it is nowhere denied that God still speaks to individuals or groups today. Devotional and biographical literature is full of situations where Christians speak of God telling them to do this or that. Christians pray that God will speak to them afresh to guide them in their choice of vocation or in their solution to a particular problem that is a burden to them. Moreover they humbly ask God to speak to them through the preaching when they meet for worship. But, of course, these cases do not constitute new or special revelation in the classical sense. There is no thought, for example, of these cases of divine speaking finding their way into the canon of Scripture. This is correct, for decisions about what constitutes this kind of personal speaking are taken within a conceptual and theological framework which already presupposes the logical primacy of special revelation. This special revelation is believed to be unique and once-for-all in classical Christian thinking. There is no question of it being repeated in the present. I think it is this conviction that lies behind the objection that there can be no divine inspiration in the present. But this in turn can only happen if divine inspiration is identified in thought and concept with divine revelation. The tacit assumption that divine inspiration, divine revelation, and divine speaking are one and the same activity has reappeared in a new guise.

A similar process is in operation when it is objected that my account of inspiration as applied to cases outside the Bible does not leave room for propositional revelation, i.e. the possibility that revelation can take the form of the communication of religious truths capable of being expressed in propositions. This is a nagging worry that makes many wary of theological proposals that do not confine inspiration to the Bible. This objection is quite unfounded. I have no antipathy to propositional revelation; in fact I believe that revelation is in part though not in whole propositional. Again what is emerging is the view that divine inspiration and divine speaking are identical. Propositional revelation, as I see it, is one kind of divine speaking that is an integral part of special revelation. Naturally, because this special revelation is contained in the Bible, there is an understandable and proper concern to see propositional revelation uniquely related to the Bible. This concern is carried over and merges with a native antipathy to alleged cases of inspiration outside the canon. But this standpoint presupposes an assumption that divine inspiration and divine speaking are identical, which is needed as a bridge from antipathy to propositional revelation outside the Bible to antipathy to divine inspiration outside the Bible. Here is fresh confirmation that many have simply failed to abandon the view that the two are in fact and in meaning identical.

Another issue that has been closely connected in the past to the topic of inspiration, is that of authority. They are like theological Siamese twins, which theologians invariably discuss in relation to each other. The point where they join is once again at the concept of revelation. In general terms Scripture is authoritive because it contains special revelation. It provides us with knowledge of God which cannot be furnished from elsewhere. It is therefore normative for Christian theology. But because inspiration has been closely related to divine speaking and this in turn has been related to special revelation, inspiration gets carried over into the area occupied by the issue of authority and vice versa. Once the meaning of revelation is prised apart from the meaning of inspiration then we no longer feel so acutely the need to explore the issue of authority when exploring the meaning of inspiration. The issue of authority belongs in fact elsewhere; it belongs to a discussion of the place of special revelation in Christian theology. Hence it will not be pursued here.[5] That I need to mention it at all is due indirectly to the confusing of divine inspiration with divine speaking.

A further and final form of this unjustified assimilation of divine speaking and divine inspiration emerges in the suspicion and hostility that is shown towards any idea of degrees of inspiration. As I argued above, it is entirely appropriate to hold that divine inspiration is a matter of degree. God can and does inspire some people more than he inspires other people. But with divine speaking it is very different. Speaking is by nature an all or nothing affair. It makes no sense to say that someone spoke to me to a greater or lesser degree. He either does speak or he does not speak; there are no degrees about it. This applies to God as much as man. It is therefore not a matter for surprise if those committed to a theology of inspiration that has failed to distinguish divine inspiration from divine speaking instinctively feel uneasy with talk of degrees of inspiration. What is happening is that their commitment to this confusion is surfacing in a new guise. Older views of inspiration are once again taking their revenge even though they have been verbally rejected.

In the course of this chapter I have attempted to provide and defend a positive account of divine inspiration. If the substance of this analysis is correct, then a coherent and serviceable doctrine has been furnished for the contemporary theologian. This doctrine preserves a concept that has a long and honourable standing in the Christian tradition. It does so by going back to the root meaning of the term and interpreting its meaning in a way that is fruitful, if not necessary, in any analysis of divine activity. Also, although by no means exclusively developed to harmonize with the nature and findings of responsible historical study of the bible, it is clearly compatible with what is generally known about the origin and content of Scripture. It is thus doubly satisfying to the Christian mind. In addition it is religiously significant and satisfying in that it permits and encourages us to seek divine inspiration for our own lives today. On this account the Christian may rightly pray that God will inspire him in meeting the varied needs of his generation just as fully as he inspired the great prophets, preachers, saints, and scholars of the past.

4

DIVINE SPEAKING AND THE AUTHORITY OF SCRIPTURE

ONE of the fundamental motives for developing a doctrine of inspiration lies in the need to secure warrants for the supreme authority of the Bible in the life of the Church. Historically, interest in inspiration can be correlated with a crisis in authority. Thus the issue first came to receive extended attention after the Reformation when the rôle of tradition became a burning theological issue. By 1577 in the famous *Formula of Concord*, there is the beginning of an interest in the doctrine of biblical inspiration. In the aftermath of the Council of Trent (1545-1563), when the Roman Catholic Church developed its doctrine in a comprehensive fashion, the issue became even more critical for Protestant theology. Protestants generally rejected the key rôle that had clearly been given to tradition alongside the bible. This in turn generated extensive concern about the warrants for locating authority in Scripture alone. The natural answer was found in the development of a doctrine of inspiration that would underscore the unique place of the Bible. It was at this time that Matthias Flacius Illyricus (1520-1575) went so far as to suggest that not only the words but even the Hebrew vowel points of the Old Testament text were inspired by God. Those who came after Flacius developed this basic conception further, drawing on sophisticated medieval distinctions about causality to do so.[1]

It is no accident that there is renewed interest in inspiration in Evangelical circles, for there is at present a crisis about authority. For some this is simply a continuation of the crisis precipitated by the Reformation. The debate, in other words, is the age-old debate about the rôle of tradition in theology. But the contemporary crisis about authority goes much deeper than this, for several reasons.

Divine Speaking and the Authority of Scripture 77

First, there is the much noted fact that almost all authority is seriously questioned today, and this radical scrutiny of authority has made much traditional thinking about the authority of Scripture look largely irrelevant and archaic. Secondly, and more specifically, there is the continuing development of critical biblical scholarship. Each new generation since the Enlightenment has added to the basic questions raised in lower and higher criticism so that the issue of the canon, once a synonym for the issue of authority, is now taken up in a field all of its own. 'Canonical Criticism' is the name now given to that discipline which gives careful attention to the origins and function of canon.[2] The sheer wealth and complexity of this material is apt to make the most stout-hearted faint when they take up the question of the warrants for treating the Bible as canon for today.

The rise of history, however, has made an even deeper impact. Principally history tends to relativize the past. The isolation of a set of documents such as those brought together in the Bible tends to be viewed as a time-bound response to certain contingencies of the past that no longer obtain.[3] Within this kind of outlook it becomes redundant to raise questions about the warrants for treating the Bible as canon. If it is raised at all the issue is not pursued with any rigour. Thus many simply commit themselves to the Bible as Scripture because the Church to which they belong does so. Where the commitment is more self-conscious, it is often made as a matter of faith exercised as a kind of 'leap in the dark'. The whole issue of the authority of Scripture is thus 'solved' by transposing it into the issue of one's community identity, or by putting it outside the range of reason altogether.

We cannot evade the matter so conveniently. The concerns that lie behind the interest in the doctrine of inspiration are entirely genuine. We surely want to know why the Bible should be given a place of unique and special significance in theology. The present crisis about authority only reveals how astute our forbears were when they bent their efforts to provide an account of inspiration that would undergird their commitment to the Bible as Scripture. Their passion and sophistication, even their excesses, are not at all to be despised. On the contrary they show the critical significance of the issue. We can go further. Behind the obsession with inspiration there lies a crucial insight that needs to be unearthed and developed to undergird the authority of Scripture in the life of the Church. In effect, the basic mistake that lies at the heart of much traditional thinking about inspiration is the kind of profound mistake that masks something of permanent value.

That mistake, we have already seen, lay in the confusing of divine inspiration with divine speaking wherein divine inspiration was treated as a complex speech-act of God. This in itself is unacceptable, but it does have a positive aspect; the emphasis on divine speaking enshrines an important suggestion about the warrants for treating the Bible as canon in theology. The essence of this suggestion is that the Bible is related in an intimate way to special divine revelation as made known in past acts of divine speaking.

I hardly need say that this is important to my basic proposals. As they stand they effectively undermine the classical warrants for the authority of the Bible. This being so, it will be natural to suppose that I am indirectly proposing that we look upon Scripture at its best as a collection of fallible human judgements that are no more worthy of acceptance than our own best insights about God. Obvious as this alternative may appear it is no part of my brief to defend it. On the contrary I want to rest the authority of the Bible neither on divine inspiration nor on wise human judgements about God but on divine revelation as made manifest in part in divine speaking. Let me explain what this means by reviewing the most important debate about the nature of revelation in recent years.

In 1952 G. Ernest Wright, the American Old Testament scholar, published a book entitled *God Who Acts: Biblical Theology in Crisis*.[4] The first part of this title became something of a slogan that summed up the general consensus in Anglo-American theology about the essence of revelation. Revelation, it was said, had been given in the 'mighty acts of God' in history. The position expressed in this slogan quickly became known as the *heilsgeschichtlich* conception of revelation.

The basic elements of this position have been set forth with characteristic lucidity by John Hick.⁵ He summarized them thus:

> This view maintains that⌈revelation consists not in the promulgation of divinely guaranteed truths but in the performance of self-revealing divine acts within human history.⌉ The locus of revelation is not propositions but events, and its content is not a body of truths about God but the 'living God' revealing himself in his actions towards man.⁶

Four theses about revelation can be distinguished here. 1. The fundamental analogy underlying revelation is the human situation where one person reveals himself to another. 2. The content of revelation is God himself, not propositions. 3. The locus of revelation is events, not propositions. 4. The mode or means of revelation is action.

This view of revelation was believed to be radically innovative. Negatively it rejected the classical view that revelation was constituted by the divine communication of a body of religious truths capable of being expressed in propositions. Positively it revised traditional conceptions of faith, the Bible, and theology. Thus, for example, where the classical view considered the Bible to be a collection of divine oracles, the new view proposed that the Bible be considered essentially as a record of the events through which God had revealed himself. What is of particular interest for our purposes, however, is the fact that the new view quite deliberately set its face against any idea of divine speaking in its conception of divine revelation. Let us explore the consequences of such a policy.

I would accept without demur the first and last theses set out above. I would agree, that is, that discourse about divine revelation should be seen as analogous to discourse about one person revealing himself to another, and that within this framework it is natural to construe the means of revelation as action. Does it follow from this that the content of revelation must be God rather than propositions, and that the locus of revelation must be events rather than propositions? The answer on both counts must be no.

Paul Helm has succinctly argued that we normally accept assertions or propositions as the bearers of the revelation of a person.⁷ He invites us to suppose that an individual, Jones, asserts such simple propositions as 'I am depressed' or 'I am going to have dinner' sincerely and truly. In making such assertions it is obvious that Jones has communicated certain propositions and that in so doing he has revealed something about himself. There is no reason why this should not apply to God. If God were to communicate certain propositions to an individual then that in itself would normally entail that God has revealed something of himself. Thus if God were to say 'I am faithful to my convenant with my people Israel', this would reveal something about God himself. It is misguided, therefore, to insist that any revelation made by asserting propositions somehow contradicts the claim that the content of revelation is God himself. Indeed such verbal revelation is crucial to our understanding of God. This emerges when we examine the view that the locus of divine revelation is events not propositions.

The issue here is not whether events in history may be classed as the locus of revelation. All sides in the discussion accept the pivotal rôle that historical events have in the Christian account of God's self-disclosure. The issue is whether events alone are the exclusive or the sufficient locus of revelation. Hick and Wright maintained that they were. The paradigm cases of revelatory events were the call of the Fathers of Israel, the deliverance from Egypt, the covenant at Sinai, the Davidic government and the life, death, and resurrection of Jesus.[8] The impression conveyed is that certain events take place in history, which can be given an entirely naturalistic explanation. These events evoke a response of 'faith' in the religious community where they are interpreted as divine acts. In the process of interpretation the community receives divine assistance, but it is far from clear what this involves. One thing it does not involve is God telling anyone what he is doing. This is the real thrust of the contention that the locus of revelation is events not propositions. If this accurately represents the new view of revelation, then it is clear that it is in serious difficulty. We can see this in what follows.

In the case of human agents we do not generally have much difficulty in deciding what they are doing. We perceive x's legs moving and see x as walking, we register sounds coming from x's mouth and simply hear x as talking, we look at x's arm going up in the air and take it as x raising his arm. We can, that is, recognize simple examples of human action instantly. That we can do this in many instances does not mean that we do not often find it difficult to decide what a particular agent is doing. This is because the same bodily movement can be seen as several different acts. Thus x moving his eyelid could be either a wink to his wife or a bid at an auction or a muscle exercise. In deciding what the agent is doing in ambiguous cases the general context can often settle the issue. Where this fails, the easiest way to find out what the agent is doing is simply to ask him. Given the agent's sincerity, his verbal response will generally be taken as the most reliable way to settle any dispute. In so far as access to the agent's speech-acts is possible, the task of removing ambiguity is immensely eased.

This is particularly crucial in disputes about the mental activity of an agent. For example, if x is sitting gazing quietly into space and we want to know whether he is doing mental arithmetic or dreaming about his girl or solving a philosophical puzzle, the best way to find out is to ask him. If he tells us, this should settle the matter.

It is also particularly crucial in cases where we want to know why the agent is doing what he is doing, i.e. in disputes about his intentions and purposes. Suppose that y has made a cake and we want to know why she did so. Her response to the question 'why did you make that cake?' will usually settle it. 'I just wanted to have fun trying out a new recipe', etc.

If the speech-acts of a human agent are often crucial in identifying his acts, they are even more crucial in the case of God. Because God does not have a body, in his case there is nothing analogous to observing his actions from his bodily behaviour straight off. It is even more important, therefore, that we have access to God's speech-acts if we are to have any idea of what he is doing, and of why he does what he does.

There are various arguments that might be deployed to defeat this conclusion. Firstly, the conclusion might be resisted by taking the bold step of insisting that God does have a body, namely the world. This is a drastic step, but even if we were prepared to take it, it would not prove very helpful. It would still leave us with the momentous task of reading God's actions off the world as a whole. Just to think of this is to discredit the argument, for no one can see the world as a whole in any way remotely analogous to the way in which one can see a human agent's body as a whole.

Secondly, the conclusion might be resisted by saying that history as a whole reveals the hand of God. Somehow when we reflect on the developmental stages that are involved in the history of mankind, when we take into account the religious, artistic, intellectual, and moral achievements of man, they give some support for the claim that in creating the world of man and nature, God intended to create a world in which man might grow to maturity and participate in creating a corporate fellowship that embraces all mankind in a bond of brotherhood. This would allow one to specify in some detail what God was intending in creation and in history without recourse to any speaking to individuals on the part of God.

It would be rash to reject out of hand the legitimacy of this view. If God has created the world of man it is surely appropriate to look to history as a whole to see if it can yield any aid in determining what he intended in the first place. Refusal to do so would be dogmatic. It would also be insensitive to the analogical character of discourse about divine creation. As it is appropriate to examine the creations of human agents to help us determine what was intended by their creators, in so far as discourse about divine creation is analogous to discourse about human creation, it is also appropriate to look to history as a whole to help us determine what God intended when he created, unless there is good reason against this procedure.

There are, however, two considerations that make this step extremely precarious. First, it is very difficult to see history synoptically in this way. Ideally what is needed is a universal history that would consist of the sum of all the significant events that have taken place in every nation from time immemorial. Such universal history simply is not available and even if it were, it is unlikely to be grasped by very many people. Perhaps only God could grasp it, but he has no need of it in determining what he intended in creating. Secondly, even if we rest content with a synoptic vision of what history we can grasp, it is a matter of substantial dispute as to how far we can see history as a history of moral and religious achievement. That there has been much intellectual and artistic achievement is beyond dispute, but whether it has been matched by moral and religious achievement is another matter. My own judgement is rather pessimistic. In so far as we can talk of history as a whole it is as much if not more a history of failure than it is a history of achievement. If we look to this, therefore, as an indicator of what God intended in creation, it might well be said to indicate the opposite. Perhaps if it supports anything in the theistic vision of the world, it supports the claim that the history of man is a history of sin and rebellion. If this is so, it would positively mislead us as an indicator of the creator's intentions.

Another way to resist the conclusion that the speech-acts of God are crucial in any attempt to determine what God intends in creation and what he has done in history can be developed by drawing on the remarks earlier made about revelation. Since the concept of revelation, like the concept of inspiration, is polymorphous, revelation is not necessarily confined to God's speech-acts. As common parlance has it, actions speak louder than words. If God creates and sustains all that is, can this activity not provide the basis for discerning his character and purposes? And if we add to this his acts in the history of Israel and in the life of Jesus then surely there is sufficient to license substantial claims about God.

The response to this argument will be made in two stages. Let it be agreed that God creates and sustains the universe. If this is so, then it is obvious that the universe is revelatory of God. As a minimum, creation reveals the intelligence and power of God. Beyond that it is a very open question how much of God is revealed by creation alone. It is doubtful if Paul goes beyond this when he writes, 'Ever since the creation of the world his invisible nature, namely his eternal power and deity, has been clearly perceived in the things that have been made.'⁹ But even if Paul does go beyond intelligence and power, the revelation available in creation will only be general in nature. Creation does not provide enough to license claims as to what God is intending for mankind when he creates.

Even such an aggressive opponent of special revelation through speech-acts as Rousseau admits this. In his account of natural religion even such general characteristics as kindness, goodness, and justice are simply necessary consequences of God's power.

> The omnipotent can only will what is good. Therefore, he who is supremely good, because he is supremely powerful, must also be supremely just; otherwise he would contradict himself; for that love of order which creates order we call goodness, and that love of order which preserves order we call justice.[10]

Beyond this, Rousseau knows nothing; further thought of God leaves him perplexed, and beyond the avoidance of thinking evil of God, he will '. . . never argue about the nature of God unless I am driven to it by the feeling of his relations with myself.'[11]

It is at this point that appeal to divine action in the history of Israel and in the life of Jesus will be made in order to supplement the revelation available in creation. As appeal to divine action in Jesus raises complex Christological issues, the second stage of the argument will be confined to considering the claim that divine action in the history of Israel adds significant content to divine action in the revelation.[12]

The problem with this can be expressed very briefly. To say that God was active in the history of Israel is to say next to nothing. To say that Napoleon was active in the history of France or Churchill was active in the history of England is to reveal very little of either Napoleon or Churchill. Nothing is in fact revealed unless the activity in which they were engaged is specified in some detail. When we know the battles Napoleon won, the diplomacy he inaugurated, the feats he accomplished at home, then and only then can we claim that events in the history of France are revelatory of Napoleon. Unfortunately, however, the *heilsgeschichtlich* view has not only been content with very vague talk about divine action in history, it has ruled out any genuine possibility of identifying what God is doing in the history of Israel. That this is so can be seen when we ask the question, how is the divine action in the history of Israel to be identified?

According to the new view the events in history through which God acts are events that have natural causes. To the unbeliever, the exodus from Egypt, for example, is just the accidental escape of a group of slaves across a treacherous marsh at the time of a strong east wind. But why should this escape be described theistically as a divine act, i.e. the divine act of God bringing slaves from Egypt? Obviously there were many other events taking place simultaneously that were also naturalistic. There were activities on Egypt's borders for example, and events in the surrounding nations, indeed events taking place in every nation across the world. Yet these events are not said to reveal God in the way in which the history of Israel does, for if they do then all events in history reveal God and we should simply appeal to the events of our own day rather than events in the history of Israel as the ground of our understanding of him.

It is insufficient in response to this challenge to reply that it was Israel's faith that saw her history as involving divine action. This is just a more religious way of saying that the Israelites interpreted the exodus as an act of God, and hence only redescribes the problem, for we now want to know what warrant they had for offering this interpretation of their history. Nor can appeal be made to the incidence of miracles, for example the dividing of the sea, for aside from any philosophical problems involved in this account of the exodus there are no such phenomena. At best the miracles are seen as the ancient Hebraic way of saying that the events of history were acts of God.

At this point it is tempting for the theologian to resort to mystery by suggesting that whether one sees an event in history as an act of God depends on 'the eye of faith'. Some people do and others do not, perhaps because of 'election', and there the matter rests. But should we be content with this? Is this not too abrupt a dismissal of the question? Is there not a missing element that is being ignored?

When we recall that a key thesis of the *heilsgeschichtlich* position was its contention that divine revelation is analogous to human revelation, it is not difficult to supply the answer. The missing element is surely the part played by speaking in most forms of personal revelation. It was this that the classical account emphasized. By telling particular people what he was doing in history, God enabled his people to grasp the revelatory significance of what took place in history. Divine action in history was thus spelled out in some detail and thereby God came to be known more fully. Without this there is nothing but confusion and ambiguity.

No doubt even with divine speaking there is still ambiguity and perhaps even confusion. And there is still plenty of room for both question and mystery when we ponder in depth what is involved in divine speaking. But none of this detracts from the key rôle that speaking has in any claim to discern divine action in history.

The traditions of Israel clearly emphasize the rôle of the prophet in the process of revelation. A fresh awareness of this has led many scholars to challenge the obsession with divine action in history. Especially important is the work of Bertil Albrektson.[13] He points out that the idea of historical events as divine manifestations is by no means unique to Israel, but occurs elsewhere in the Near East. Two of his concluding remarks are relevant here. First, if revelation is restricted to events, then its content must be restricted: 'The events themselves are naturally mute in many vital respects. they may . . . reveal the deity's power, his anger or pleasure, but they cannot possibly disclose his reasons or causes, purposes and intentions.'[14] Secondly, in order to gain access to God's intentions and purposes a communication from God is necessary. We need not just a revelation in history but also a revelation about history: '. . . Israel's knowledge of God's purposes in history is not obtained through history but through the divine word about history.'[15] What may be unique about Israel's history is in fact the content of the word the prophets brought.

. . . it is a common belief that the deity speaks to man, and prophets claiming to reveal divine messages are known outside Israel. But the content of this revelation is in several respects unique. It is here that we learn of YHWH's purposes and intentions, his true nature and the innermost thoughts of his heart, his gifts and his claims which make him different from all the other gods of the ancient Near East.[16]

What applies to prophets like Jeremiah applies equally well to an apostle like Paul. What makes Paul important is not just his nearness to the events he interprets but his claim to be the recipient of special revelation. His message about the cross is nothing less than a word from God disclosing what could not have been known in any depth without special divine action in his own life. God had spoken directly to him; it was as simple as that.[17]

It might be objected that this whole approach to divine speaking is too 'supernaturalistic'. Statements of the form 'God spoke to x', should be interpreted in a very different way. Rather than read them as claims about direct acts of God in the world, we should see them as statements about the interpretation of human experience. They describe our response to general divine action in human experience. As G. W. H. Lampe puts it: 'What may make us call an event an act of God, or cause us to find God disclosed in it, is our reaction to it, that is to say the effect which it has on us.'[18]

In reacting to the divine in human experience, some people are more sensitive than others. In interpreting their response to God, expressions such as 'x thought' or 'x was convinced' are too weak to describe their experience. To say 'God spoke to x' is a much more fitting description of its vivid and striking character. In the development of the Jewish and Christian tradition such people as the prophets were recognized as possessing this special sensitivity to God's activity in the world. Their experience was accepted as 'classical' and they were accorded a rôle analogous to that of the expert in other spheres. The establishment of these reference points of revelatory experience was a long process and involved the application of several criteria of assessment.

An advantage which this alternative analysis possesses is that it allows us to abandon discourse about divine intervention. This is invaluable, for

Events as such do not seem to be divisible into those which are acts of God and those which are not. The Christian may indeed believe that nothing happens which God does not either positively will or at any rate permit, and in this sense all events may be called acts of God; but there seem to be no events which, by virtue of some intrinsic quality that distinguishes them from others, compel us whether we are believers or not to describe them as acts of God. Any event may in certain circumstances lend itself to being so interpreted. No event, on the other hand, need be understood as an act of God in any but the general sense indicated above; in no case is some other interpretation excluded by the observable facts themselves.[19]

For those who believe that the character of historical investigation rules out discourse about divine intervention in the world, this analysis of divine speaking is a welcome relief. I do not consider, however, that it is adequate.

First, it sets unreasonably high standards for individuating acts of God in the world. There may indeed be no intrinsic quality about certain events that would lead us to claim that they were brought about directly by God. But this is also true of many events brought about by human agents. We are often convinced that an agent brought about an event only after much deliberation, and are convinced not by one consideration but by many taken together. In none of these cases can we exclude all other interpretations although we may make them look implausible and strained.

Secondly, it is insufficient to treat performances or acts of God merely as a culturally conditioned way of talking about God's positive willing or permitting of events. The Christian indeed accepts that all events, even the most evil of events, can only take place because of the prior creative and sustaining activity of God. But this is radically different from saying that any event is an act of God, or indeed that it should legitimately be called an act of God. The event of Hitler exterminating the Jews could not have happened had God not permitted it. But it is not just odd but wrong to say that this event was an act of God. Other conditions than the mere fact that God permits it must be satisfied if this is to be allowed. To treat 'acts of God' as another way of expressing general divine permission just ignores this fact.

Thirdly, treating discourse about divine speaking as another way of expressing claims about our response to human experience comes perilously close to denying human freedom in response to God. It is indeed true to claim that to say 'God spoke to x' is a human interpretation of experience, but this is a general truth about all human discourse about experience. When a prophet says 'God spoke to me', he is interpreting his experience and may well be wrong in his interpretation. But this does not entail the view that all that was taking place was his response, and that God was not acting directly. Indeed we can logically distinguish three separate acts in the process of revelation and response. First, there is the act of God in speaking; secondly, there is the act of recognition on the part of the recipient, and thirdly, there is the response of the recipient to the revelation. For revelation to have taken place the first two need to be described, since revelation is an achievement verb, but we can well describe the act and its recognition without also describing the kind of response that revelation initiates. It is surely at this third stage that the element of freedom is to be primarily located. On Lampe's analysis of revelation, the response seems compelled by definition: 'It is an oversimplification to say that the response is evoked by the revelation, for the sense of a compulsion to respond is integral to the experience; it is of its essence, and it makes the occasion revelatory.'[20]

Fourthly, it is quite proper to claim that the recognition of divine action in either creation as a whole or in particular events in history will require sensitivity and insight. But more is required than just sensitivity and human insight if God's intentions and purposes are to be known. As we have seen, it is difficult to see how these can be read off the world or history by even the most sensitive of hearts and minds. To be sure, they may give us some insight into what God intends, but the content of God's intentions that can be read off the world in this way falls far short of what would be available if he had revealed himself by word and deed and not just by his general creative activity. Divine speaking and human sensitivity together bring about divine revelation. The latter will be necessary to recognize the former, but the former too is necessary if revelation in anything but the most general form is to emerge.

The emphasis on divine speaking that pervades so much of the Bible, therefore, is of the profoundest significance.

Admittedly it is possible to undervalue the rôle of history in revelation if too much attention is given to divine speaking, but this is unlikely to happen in our day. More probably Evangelicals will continue to emphasize the importance of divine speaking in order to buttress their insistence on inerrancy. Happily, however, those who have been awakened to the need to distinguish between divine speaking and divine inspiration will resist such endeavours.

It is to be hoped that they will be encouraged in this by the main point of this chapter. The central argument has been that divine speaking to agents like prophets and apostles is an extremely important source of access to God's intentions and purposes. It is through God's word that we in part discover his action in history for the saving of mankind. Since this word together with his action is recorded and enshrined in the Bible, we have good cause to approach it not just with respect and in earnest but with reverence and in prayer. In a word, we have secure warrants for treating the Bible as canon in the life of the Church today.

5

EXEGETICAL CONSIDERATIONS

Up to this point I have identified a need and attempted to meet it. We need to rethink and reformulate the doctrine of the inspiration of the Bible. Recent theology generally and recent Evangelical theology in particular have failed to provide an adequate account of inspiration. In chapter three I attempted to redeem this situation. I offered an analysis of inspiration as applied to the Bible that is contemporary, coherent, and credible.

In this chapter I approach our theme from a different angle. Here I turn to exegesis, and intend to show that my position does full justice to the classical texts of the Bible on inspiration. I have two aims in this. On the one hand I want to suggest that the classical texts count decisively against the standard orthodoxy that has already been rejected on conceptual grounds. On the other I want to show that the view I have outlined is fully in harmony with the self-same texts. Whether it is required in any strict sense by these texts is a matter I shall not pursue here.

It may seem odd, if not unwise, to leave exegetical considerations to this late point in our analysis of inspiration. After all, it might be said, it is a mark of Evangelical theology that it be loyal to the Bible, hence exegetical matters should have been introduced earlier. This comment is simplistic in at least three ways.

First, that exegetical considerations appear relatively late does not show that they are being treated theologically as secondary. Chronology and significance are not to be identified. In my own pilgrimage to the present proposals it is impossible to determine when the standard orthodoxy ceased to satisfy in the field of exegesis. It certainly happened at an early stage of my thinking. But this does not matter. What matters is that any proposed theory of inspiration deal adequately with the whole range of relevant evidence. The chronology of the discussion is a matter of literary convenience.

Secondly, it is not sufficiently recognized that the interpretation of Scripture involves more than exegesis as that is traditionally understood. There are conceptual, even philosophical, dimensions to religious discourse that can be easily overlooked in the exegesis of the Bible. We need to remember this in order to guard against an exclusivist emphasis on knowledge of the original languages.

Lastly, this comment ignores the extent to which the articulation of a doctrine of inspiration is a human activity. As such it will, of course, rely on and be built upon exegetical conclusions. But these conclusions are human conclusions; they are not a matter of direct divine revelation. This is why I am reluctant to claim that any theory of inspiration, including my own, is strictly required by Scripture. There is more to the construction of a theory than the simple appeal of the Bible; we are engaged in more than exegesis. This is equally suggested by the fact that a doctrine of inspiration is not purely a personal or individual affair. One does not begin from scratch and develop it alone *ab initio*; one works from within a theological tradition and that tradition is also a human tradition. This is of enormous significance and many Evangelicals have been blind to this, as we shall see in the next chapter. For now I simply want to stress that although exegetical considerations are crucial in my view in any doctrine of inspiration, they are not the only considerations. There are philosophical and historical dimensions that are also of importance and obsession with exegesis can all too easily lead us to ignore these to our cost.

When we actually turn to the relevant material, one of the most striking features about it is that there are relatively few texts which deal explicitly with the topic of inspiration. Two invariably occur in the literature: 2 Tim. 3:16 and 2 Peter 1:21. In fact of these two texts only the first deals directly with the topic of inspiration. Furthermore, 2 Timothy cannot on any account be considered a central book in the Bible. Important as it is in certain respects it cannot stand on a par with Romans, Galatians, or Hebrews, not to speak of the Gospels. This scarcity of material and its confinement to a marginal book is remarkable. At the very least it should prompt us to question whether a doctrine of inspiration should be made the foundation-stone of Evangelical theology, for Evangelical theology must be true not just to the letter of Scripture but to its proportions and emphases.

The predictable reply to this will be to insist that the standard orthodoxy is not founded on 2 Tim. 3:16 and 2 Peter 1:21 alone. Warfield, for example, held that there was a wealth of exegetical evidence to support his view. He uses the analogy of an avalanche to express his confidence in this regard. For him there were not scores but hundreds of texts to rest upon, or rather there were hundred of texts under which one would be buried should one face the full force of the avalanche. 'What a pity it is that we cannot see and feel the avalanche of texts beneath which we may lie hopelessly buried, as clearly as we may see and feel an avalanche of stones!'[1] This is, of course, ridiculous and gross exaggeration. There is no such avalanche at all. There are in fact three general groups of texts. There are the classical texts of 2 Tim. 3:16 and 2 Peter 1:21. There are those texts that reveal the attitude of Jesus to the Old Testament. Finally there are those texts where little distinction is made between what God says and what Scripture says. These constitute the central material to be covered. Let us look at each of these in turn.

Of all the texts 2 Tim. 3:16 is the most widely used as a proof-text of inspiration. 'All scripture is inspired by God and profitable for teaching, for reproof, for correction, for training in righteousness that the man of God may be complete, equipped for every good work.' Leaving aside the irrelevant issue of how to translate the opening phrase, let us note what this text actually says. For a start the text simply says that Scripture is inspired by God. There is no detailed theory of inspiration as such here. There is no mention of Scripture being word for word the very words of God. There is no mention of inerrancy; this inference is not drawn by the writer. This is not to say that Scripture is said to have no didactic content. It clearly is profitable for teaching, for reproof, for correction. But this is a far cry from inerrancy.

Nor is inerrancy entailed by what is said about the teaching function of Scripture. Indeed the inferences that Paul draws are very modest compared to the highly specific and inflated ones that have been drawn from the concept. The didactic content of Scripture is primarily theological. It aims to teach the will of God rather than impart detailed information about nature or history. Furthermore, although Scripture clearly is didactic, its ultimate content is spiritual and moral. The whole context of the chapter makes this clear. Scripture aims to make the man of God complete, equipped for every good work. In other words Scripture is centrally to be seen not so much as a book of divine truths but more as a means of grace.

It is also significant that Paul is not writing about the original autographs. He is referring to the Scriptures that were there and then used by Timothy and by those who brought him to faith. We know as a matter of fact that these differed from the original autographs. Timothy would have used as a Jew the Greek translation of the Old Testament and we know that this differed from the original Hebrew text. In other words Paul refers to present copies and translations rather than past original manuscripts when he writes of inspiration. And when he speaks of inspiration our present translations rightly use the present tense ('*is* inspired by God'), a move that is vindicated by the tenses that follow in the verse. The whole thrust of 2 Tim. 3:16 then goes clearly against the standard orthodoxy; yet it is wholly in harmony with the alternative proposal developed earlier.

2 Peter 1:21 has even less to say on inspiration than 2 Tim. 3:16. '. . . no prophecy ever came by the impulse of man, but men moved by the Holy Spirit spoke from God'. Again let us note how modest the claim is. There is no mention of the view that the very words of the Bible are given by God. It is men who speak, men who are moved by God. We are not even told that they are addressed by God. The key point made is that God took the initiative in directing the prophets. God moved them to prophesy – what they said did not come from the impulse of man. Beyond this 2 Peter 1:21 is silent. Here there is no mention of original autographs, no mention of divine speaking, no mention of

Exegetical Considerations

inerrancy and no inflated claims about the character of Scripture as a whole. Those who profess to see more are importing into the text human tradition that goes beyond what Scripture teaches. Whereof the text does not speak, thereof we should be silent.

When we turn to those texts that deal with the attitude of Jesus to Scripture we enter much more controversial and difficult territory. There need be no apology, however, for covering this terrain. We have every right to appeal to Jesus in our account of the status of Scripture. Jesus is surely uniquely normative in Christian thinking. But we must be very sensitive at this point. James Barr has registered a timely protest when he insists that the personal loyalty of Christians to Jesus should not be used to force people into 'fundamentalist' positions on historical and literary matters. As he rightly points out there is in this a distasteful distortion of the proper proportions of the Christian faith.[2] There may also be a failure to acknowledge that the evidence must be a matter of sensitive theological and historical judgement.

It requires sensitive theological judgement because any argument must rely on central theological conclusions as to who Jesus was and is. Without these the appeal to Jesus will lack force. It requires sensitive historical judgement because of the complex historical questions that are raised by the New Testament documents. The danger is that this whole process will be abruptly short-circuited by a direct appeal to the Christian's loyalty to Christ that simplistically ignores the manifold grounds for this commitment. As well as this, there is the added danger that we shall interpret this loyalty in restrictive and narrow terms. We must recognize that it is one thing to be loyal to Christ but it is another thing to be loyal to someone's interpretation of loyalty to Christ. We should resist coercion at the latter level. We must in turn be aware of harsh, judgemental criticism that would equate loyalty to our beliefs with loyalty to Christ. Evangelicals especially need to attend to this.

That said, there is no need for either theological or historical alarmism concerning Jesus. I myself do not share the fashionable scepticism about the incarnation and about the historic Christ. As to the classical texts in the Gospels that have been discussed in connection with inspiration, let us examine them as they stand and see where they lead. Let us summarize to begin with the general approach to Scripture adopted by Jesus.

There is very general agreement that Jesus had a very high view of the Old Testament. It is clear from even a cursory reading of the Gospels that he was steeped in its concepts and content. He had been exposed to it from childhood, he appealed to it in disputes with opponents, he drew on it to cope with temptation, and he used it to expound and explain his life and ministry. All this is not a matter of dispute. Indeed one expects such an attitude given what Jews and Christians believe about the special revelation that was given to Israel in history and prophecy. If the Old Testament contains the recorded revelation of God in the past, it is only natural and logical that it will be taken as authoritative in religious matters.

In this Jesus is in line with the Judaism of his time. The evidence of the Gospels dovetails with what we would expect from his historical background. With his fellow-Jews, Jesus held that the Old Testament is of paramount religious significance. It had a status that was high and a position that was authoritative.

At this point some are likely to become edgy about the broad terms in which I have sketched the attitude of Jesus to the Old Testament. Yet what has been sketched is as much as can be said from general historical considerations concerning the Judaism out of which Jesus emerged. History does not allow us to go further. What was settled as Hans von Campenhausen has argued, was the idea of a normative collection of sacred writings.[3] That there was a canon is clearly attested as early as the second century BC. Beyond this it is impossible to define with precision the concept of Scripture held by the Jews at the time of Jesus. The relevant sources are too scarce to go further. In any case various parties within Judaism held divergent views on the subject.

It is equally difficult to be precise about the concept of Scripture held universally by Christians in the early period. That Scripture is normative is obvious and agreed. God was uniquely related to the production of Scripture; this too is probably agreed. But this does not in itself constitute a theory of inspiration. On the contrary there are no credal formulations in the early Church on inspiration that are on a level with the classical formulations, say, of Christological doctrine. There are, to be sure, various suggestions in the Fathers but, as Wiles points out, it is difficult to find one theory that is sufficiently representative to deserve description as the dominent theory.[4]

It is important to bear this in mind when we consider Jesus' attitude to Scripture. There is a grave danger that we will read back our own theories into the texts under review. We need to be sensitive to the rich diversity of the Jewish past. In particular we need to distinguish sharply between seeing the Bible as normative and seeing the Bible as verbally inspired. For epistemological reasons some Evangelicals construe these as either identical or logically connected. For the present we simply note that general historical considerations reveal that those who preceded Jesus in Judaism and those who came after him in the early Church did not have an agreed theory of inspiration. Jesus is bounded on either side by religious thinkers who accepted with him that Scripture is normative but did not as a whole subscribe to the precise conception of inspiration that constitutes current orthodoxy.

Be that as it may, some are likely to be unimpressed. General historical evidence, it might be said, must bear much less weight than the concrete examination of specific texts in the gospels. These are decisive, and it will be suggested that they count in the opposite direction to which I am pointing.

The main weakness with this is the momentous silence about inspiration on the part of Jesus in the Gospels. There is no point in the Gospels where Jesus speaks explicitly of the inspiration of the Bible. Nor is there any reference to the original autographs. Jesus, like Paul, refers to copies and translations, not to original autographs when he comments on Scripture. Nor is there any explicit reference to inerrancy. There is not a single text that speaks plainly and explicitly on these matters. This is surely astonishing. If inspiration was so important to him, then we could at least have had a clear indication of this. Indeed once we remember that many of the texts simply reflect a traditional Jewish respect for Scripture as normative and canonical, there are surprisingly few verses to review.

Let us take the words of Jesus in John 10:35, where, after appealing to Psalm 82:6, Jesus, says that 'Scripture cannot be broken'. Is this an explicit appeal to an inerrant autograph? I think it is an exaggeration to go this far. The context makes it clear that the argument used by Jesus is essentially *ad hominem*. Jesus is drawing on classical Jewish respect for the Old Testament to rebut the charge of blasphemy that had been levelled against him. The primary concern of the passage is not to articulate a position on inspiration but to defend the relation that exists between Jesus and the Father. In this controversy with the Jews Jesus is content to appeal to premises that his opponents cannot deny. We simply cannot extrapolate from this to an elaborate theory of inspiration.

By far the most important text is Matthew 5:17-18. It throws great light on the whole attitude of Jesus to the Old Testament. It begins with a very positive statement of it: 'think not that I have come to abolish the law and the prophets'. It proceeds to state the relation of the work of Jesus to them: 'I have come not to abolish but to fulfil.' The next verse re-emphasizes the abiding significance of the law and the prophets. 'For truly I say to you, till heaven and earth pass away not an iota, not a dot will pass from the law until all is accomplished.'

The general context of this material is clearly ethical; its place in the sermon on the mount is sufficient to guarantee this. Not surprisingly, therefore, it is a key text in discussions about the relation between Jesus and the Old Testament law. It has in this regard often featured as a proof that Jesus in no way intended to abrogate the moral law of the Old Testament. Rather, he endorsed its demands, and his own ethical teaching must be seen as a supplement to the moral content of the Old Testament.

Because of this general ethical intent we must be cautious in using this material to work out Jesus' view of inspiration. The latter is at least one remove from the main point of the passage. But the two are connected. On the one hand, those committed to inerrancy tend to take the view that Jesus endorsed all of the ethical content of the Old Testament. This is entirely logical. If the Bible is inerrant then the ethical content of the Old Testament is inerrant and Jesus, being the Son of God, must as a matter of logic adhere to it. One could circumvent this, but it requires great sophistication to do so, and I shall not attempt it here. On the other hand, if it can be shown that this passage suggests a qualified appropriation of the Old Testament on the part of Jesus, then it goes a long way to establishing that more has been read into this material in regard to inspiration than has been read out of it by proper exegesis. Let us explore this by concentrating on the view that this passage shows that Jesus wholly endorsed the moral law of the Old Testament.

The first thing to notice is that this text says nothing about the moral law of the Old Testament as such. Jesus does not draw a distinction between the moral, ceremonial, and civil laws of the Old Testament, as we might. He may do so elsewhere but he does not do so here. Jesus speaks of all the law, indeed he is quite specific; he speaks of the law and the prophets, and he is concerned with all of these.

His attitude to this material is twofold. Negatively he did not come to abolish it. As verse 18 puts it, 'not an iota, not a dot will pass from the law until all is accomplished'. Positively he came to fulfil it. He came to fulfil the law and the prophets. Everything hinges on how we interpret these two verbs, 'abolish' and 'fulfil'.

Let us take 'abolish' first. It might seem that Jesus' claim not to abolish the law must be taken to mean that at no time was obedience to the entire law to cease. This is the basis for the use of this text as a support for inerrancy. But there are two difficulties in this interpretation. First, it suggests a time set when the iotas and dots of the law will pass away, that is, when all is accomplished. Secondly, no Christian actually accepts in practice this interpretation. Clearly, Christians do not obey wide tracts of the law. They no longer keep the ceremonial or the civil law; nor do they keep the law of the Sabbath in the sense specified here, as Seventh Day Adventists remind us. It is because of this that sophisticated distinctions between various elements in the law have been invented. These are alien to what is explictly stated here, for Jesus speaks of all the law, down to its iotas and dots. For these reasons I suggest that we cannot take opposition to abolishing the law to mean that obedience to all the law is enjoined for ever. Where this interpretation is surely correct, however, is in its stress on obedience to the law. Jesus does enjoin continued adherence to the law, and yet he makes one critical qualification: this is to last only until all is accomplished. By this I take to mean that the law stands whole and entire until he has completed all that the Father intended him to achieve in his life and ministry. After that there is a new convenant and a new Israel of God.

How well does this fit with the other verb used to describe Jesus' relation to the law and the prophets, namely 'fulfil'? Many have taken this to mean simply that Jesus himself fulfilled the law, in keeping it down to its last detail, by giving it a deeper and more exacting meaning and by reinforcing its moral demands on the disciples. This is plausible but unacceptable. The text does not say that Jesus kept all the law: it says he fulfils the law. Moreover the introduction of a distinction between the moral and non-moral parts of the law should make us sceptical of this whole approach to the meaning of 'fulfil'. We are smuggling in material that is alien to the passage as a whole. Is there a satisfactory alternative interpretation?

The verb in the original, πληρόω, when used non-literally means 'to fill with a content', 'to fill completely'. This gives a clear clue as to how we should proceed. Jesus fulfils the law, he completes the law and the prophets, not just in the sense that he gives a deeper understanding of these, but in the sense that he fully expresses their inner intention and purpose. The whole point of the law and the prophets was to being about right relationships with God and to make Israel a holy nation. This they did to some degree. In Jesus, however, this purpose is fulfilled to the highest degree. In him God's will is fully actualized; in him the true spirit of the law and the prophets achieves its fullest expression. When he has accomplished all, the law and the prophets are not abolished but transcended. He is the true norm of God's will

Exegetical Considerations

for which the law and the prophets have been preparing. These are not cast aside entirely. What Jesus endorses is to be obeyed out of loyalty to him. Moreover they are needed for understanding of what Jesus is and does. But they are provisional and relative. They have value in that they express the will of God, but their value is relative because they do not express it in the complete and full way accomplished in Jesus. They must be read and evaluated in the light of Christ, the one who is truly Lord over us as Christians.

This interpretation makes very good sense of Jesus' own relation to the law as revealed by his life and deeds. There is here too a qualified appropriation at work. On the one hand Jesus is a Jew who keeps the law in a conventional manner. He participates in its worship; he adheres to its precepts; he acknowledges that the law and the prophets express the will of God. Hence he appeals to Scripture in controversy, in temptation, and in explaining the purpose of his ministry. Moreover, he draws on the weightier matters of the law and insists that there can be no abrogation of them. Here there is genuine continuity with the law and the prophets. The exegesis of Jesus at this point is profound and exacting. It does not destroy the law. As Hans von Campenhausen says:

On the contrary, if the law is understood in accordance with its deepest meaning and with the mind of God and His Messiah, it genuinely affirms it and puts it into practice for the first time. This definitive, perfect understanding of the Law was taught by Jesus and adopted by Christians; and it was to make this point that Matthew coined the exaggerated formula, that Jesus had not come to destroy the Law but to fulfil it.[5]

On the other hand there is also clear discontinuity with the law in the life of Jesus. He selects one part as more binding than another part, as in his comments on divorce (Matt. 10:1-12). He appeals to the law-breaking of David to justify the actions of his disciples when they are accused of breaking the Sabbath (Matt. 7:1-23). He challenges not just Rabbinic additions to the law in the matter of oaths and retaliation but the very laws of the Old Testament itself (Matt. 5:33-37). Shining through these incidents is the radical authority and newness of Jesus. With him there is indeed a new covenant that transcends the old rather than just extends it. In his words and deeds there is a ringing authority that needs no exegesis to support it. He himself is the new wine for which the old bottles are quite inadequate (Matt. 5:37-39). There is a real sense then, in which, he is the unique locus of the will of God. As such he must transcend and supersede the relative expression of that will as it was given in the law and the prophets.

We have travelled a long way to deal with a passage that has taxed the minds of the great exegetes. It has not been in vain. On the one side, surely it is clear by now that this passage does not show that Jesus held the Old Testament to be inerrant. To press this from the text of Matt. 5:17-18 is to over-interpret. Jesus did not hold to a flat view of the Old Testament. He certainly held that it expressed the will of God, but this must be read sensitively. There is a genuine dialectical relation between Jesus and the Old Testament; there is both a 'yes' and a 'no' in his use of it, rather than an unqualified 'yes'. On the other side this qualified use of the Old Testament is much more in harmony with the account of inspiration developed in the previous chapter. That account can accommodate without strain the kind of qualified approach to the Old Testament that is exhibited in the teaching and action of Jesus.

Before we leave the material that reveals the attitude of Jesus to Scripture there is one more piece of evidence to examine. In doing so we can touch an issue that is widely discussed in the literature on inspiration, namely the question of the inspiration of the New Testament. It is recognized that none of the texts explored so far deal directly with this issue. Two moves are often made to redress the situation.

First, the verbal inspiration of the Old Testament is established by conventional texts such as we have examined, and it is then argued or suggested that this is the meaning of inspiration that must be predicated of the New Testament. Secondly, appeal is made to John's Gospel to show that Jesus promises to lead the apostles into the whole truth. This coupled with arguments that purport to establish that this promise was fulfilled in the work of the apostles, is taken as the full endorsement by Jesus of the verbal inspiration of the New Testament. Both these arguments enshrine important insights but they fail to substantiate the point at issue.

The first fails simply because the conventional texts do not establish the verbal inspiration of the Old Testament. Certainly the texts examined so far do not do so. In fact what the early Church takes over into its theology of Scripture as regards its approach to the New Testament is the idea of a normative body of literature. It is this that in part leads it to collect an authoritative canon. It is this insight that the argument has misrepresented by assuming that it involves subscribing to verbal inspiration in the desired sense.

The second argument is also unsuccessful. It appeals to such verses as John 17:7 and John 14:25 to license the proposal that the Holy Spirit will give the apostles the exact words in which they are to write. In this regard much is made of the plural in John 17:8, '. . . for the words. . . '. What this argument rests on is the much neglected insight that the Holy Spirit did indeed lead the early Church into the truth about Jesus. In a genuine sense the apostles were recipients of special revelation. Without this they could not have adequately appreciated the purposes of God achieved in Jesus. This is an important matter that I cannot explore here. Suffice it to say that, as I see it, there is revelation both before and after the coming of Jesus which is indispensable. In a very real sense the Church is built on the foundation of the prophets and apostles. But this in no way amounts to the thesis that the New Testament is verbally inspired or inerrant. To suggest this is to confuse afresh revelation and inspiration. We are back at the basic conceptual confusion that has bedevilled the discussion on inspiration for so long.

Aside from the lack of positive evidence to establish the verbal inspiration of the New Testament, there is one piece of evidence that counts decisively against it. It is to be found in 1 Cor. 7:10, 12, 25. Here Paul makes a clear distinction between his own opinion and the word of the Lord. We have, that is, material in the New Testament which on its own clear and specific understanding cannot be construed as being given word for word by God. We must conclude therefore that the New Testament is not verbally inspired.

If, however, we consider inspiration in the light in which I have depicted it, there is no real problem in establishing the inspiration of the New Testament. If God has revealed himself uniquely in Jesus and if he has revealed the significance of this to chosen apostles, then through this very activity, as well as through his personal dealings with the apostles, God will have inspired them and others to record, collect, and edit the traditions that are now enshrined in the New Testament. There need be no prolonged debate about this once the nature of inspiration as sketched earlier is grasped. To be sure, there will be debate about the classical revelation I have appealed to at this point. This is as it should be, for revelation raises complex questions in both theology and philosophy. But in a discussion about inspiration this takes us beyond our terms of reference. All that matters is that it can be seen quite clearly that once one accepts the classical commitments concerning revelation under the new covenant, the question of the inspiration of the New Testament can be settled without undue perplexity. The general logic of the argument is both perspicious and impeccable. Given that God has revealed himself as specified and given that those who received and passed on this revelation were in intimate communion with God, *ipso facto* they will be inspired to record and preserve that which is of such importance to us all.

We are left with a third and final set of verses in our review of the exegetical evidence related to inspiration, those verses where New Testament writers cite Old Testament material as if they were direct uterances of God. Warfield devotes a long article to this topic and, drawing attention to the two crucial classes of verses involved, summarizes the argument succinctly as follows:

In one of these classes of passages the Scriptures are spoken as if they were God; in the other, God is spoken of as if He were the Scriptures: in the two together, God and the Scriptures are brought into such conjunction as to show that in point of directness of authority no distinction was made between them.[6]

An example of the former class is Rom. 9:17 (For the scripture says to Pharaoh, 'I have raised you up . . .'). An

Exegetical Considerations

example of the second class is Hebrews 3:7 (Therefore as the Holy Spirit says 'Today, when you hear . . .'). In addition to this there are those passages that introduce quotations by the subjectless λέγει or φησί, it being taken for granted that the subject to be supplied is God. Examples are Rom. 9:15 (For he says to Moses, 'I will have mercy . . .'), and Heb. 8:5 (for when Moses was about to erect the tent, he was instructed by God, saying, 'see that you make everything . . .').

The question to be raised is simply this: do these citations and formulae of citations support the view that the Old Testament was verbally inspired and inerrant in its original autographs? The answer must be a clear and unqualified 'no'. Aside from the fact that these verses make no mention of either inerrancy or the original autographs, they key point to be made is that if we do rely on them they support not a theory of divine inspiration but a theory of divine dictation. They support the view that the content of the Bible was spoken by God rather than that it was inspired by God. This is patently clear from the way in which Warfield expresses his argument. Citing a number of relevant passages, he comments thus:

> It is not God, however, in whose mouth these sayings are placed in the text of the Old Testament. They are the words of others, recorded in the text of scripture as spoken to or of God. They could be attributed to God only through such habitual identification, in the minds of the writers, of the text of scripture that it became natural to use the terms "God says" when what was really intended was "Scripture, the Word of God, says". The two sets of passages, together, thus show an absolute identification, in the minds of these writers of 'scripture' with the *speaking* God.

This emphasis on the speaking God runs throughout Warfield's treatment of the subject. If he really wants to follow the logic of his argument he should recognize that he has proved too much. This material, as Warfield uses it, really supports a theory more of divine dictation than of divine inspiration. Warfield fails to see this for obvious reasons. With others he has confused divine inspiring with divine speaking, so he is quite happy to argue for the former by arguing merely for the latter. For him texts that refer to divine speaking are revelant *simpliciter* to divine inspiration. Moreover, he has failed to recognize that divine dictating is just one form of divine speaking. So if you provide an argument for one you automatically provide an argument for the other unless you trouble to distinguish the two with some care. To argue that all of the Bible is spoken by God is no different from arguing that it is dictated by God. Because Warfield does not see this, he fails to recognize that in using the formulae of citation as he does, he is really proving far too much.

This is sufficient to undermine the standard deployment of the third class of texts to support verbal inspiration. However, we do not have to leave the matter here. A much more satisfactory interpretation of these verses is available and there are other considerations that confirm our own position on inspiration.

The best way to construe these passages is to see them as expressing traditional Jewish respect for the content of the Old Testament canon. We should not read any more into them than this. Indeed we can understand why the New Testament writers in citing the Old Testament would naturally use formulae that refer to God as speaking. It is central to their conviction that God has spoken in the past – he spoke in the events of history and he spoke in his word to the prophets of old. It is altogether understandable that this should be reflected in their references to passages of the very Scriptures that enshrine this revelation in written form. For them the Scriptures are the Word of God, the oracles of God. They record what God has spoken in many and varied ways to his people. They therefore quite naturally quote them as being spoken by God.

I suspect that what is happening here is that the part is being used to stand for the whole. Recognizing that God has spoken his word and that this is recorded in the Old Testament they happily talk of all of it being the Word of God. There is a clear parallel in the use of the term 'law' to stand not just for the legal parts of the Old Testament but for all of it.[8] In neither case should this convention be pressed to the point where all of the canon is viewed as containing exclusively either legal material or verbal revelation. However, it is not crucial to my case that this should be the underlying process that is operating. What matters is that we see the formulae of citation as a fitting expression of the deep respect there is for the canon of the Old Testament. To press them further is to exaggerate their significance and relevance.

This reading of these verses is borne out by two other considerations. First, it is supported by the fact that the formulae of citation are particularly numerous in the book of Hebrews, the most Jewish epistle in the New Testament. They occur elsewhere, of course, but less frequently. Secondly it is borne out by the fact that, in the actual quoting of the Old Testament, the New Testament writers exercise extensive freedom. A careful study of the relevant material will show that sometimes they quote the Septuagint, sometimes the original Hebrew, sometimes a combination of the two, sometimes an unique translation. There is no slavish commitment to the original autographs such as one might expect if they were so crucial. The formulae, therefore, are not to be taken in the exact and wooden way that is central to their use in arguments to establish the verbal inspiration of the Bible.

Our examination of the classical biblical passages is now complete. To be sure, not all the relevant texts have been covered. However, our exegesis of the crucial material reveals that it counts decisively against the standard orthodoxy on inspiration in recent years. The alternative theory developed above is in a much better position, for it is fully in harmony with what the Bible has to say about inspiration. It attempts to articulate what inspiration is as applied to the Bible in a way that is fully compatible with what the Bible itself has to say about this matter. It should therefore be welcomed by those who take Scripture seriously as a norm in theology.

Despite this it would be utopian to expect that most Evangelicals will welcome the central thesis of this book with enthusiasm. Even though it purports to be based upon Scripture there will be a certain degree of hesitation, if not scepticism. One might in turn be dismissive of this reaction. What it reveals, one might argue, is a true commitment not to Scripture but to the traditions of the recent elders. There may be some truth in this, for it is one thing to be committed in theory to Scripture and another thing to be committed in practice. In this respect Evangelicals are no less human than others. Let each examine himself and judge accordingly.

7

POSTSCRIPT

AT the beginning of this study I made no secret of the fact that I was writing from within an Evangelical tradition. Those who see nothing good coming from this direction will by now have gone elsewhere for food for thought. Those confused by the term 'Evangelical' may have tarried in the hope of receiving some light on what it might mean. On the other hand those who felt very sure that they knew what this term means may find it strange that I should want to associate it with the contents of this study. In particular, many Evangelicals may be perplexed if not annoyed to be offered an account of inspiration that is very different from what they believe. My hope is that they are sufficiently aware of the present crisis about inspiration to have stayed the course and read with care what I have argued.

My thesis is simple. Evangelicals need to rethink and revise their ideas on the inspiration of the Bible. The standard orthodoxy developed by Warfield is beset with manifold difficulties that cannot be overcome by tinkering here and there with its content. We need a fresh and positive start. We require a genuine alternative that is self-consciously developed to meet the intellectual needs of the present. It is this that I have sought to furnish. My aim has been to set forth an account of inspiration that is intellectually viable and religiously valuable.

I trust it has been obvious that my proposal is intended as Evangelical in character. Those sensitive to this dimension will have seen this reflected in my attempt to interact in a serious manner with the standard orthodoxy of the recent past among Evangelicals, in my confessed desire to speak to the crisis that exists at present on inspiration, and, most of all, in my concern to do justice to the biblical material on inspiration. I write out of gratitude to the Evangelical tradition and I write as one who gladly identifies with that tradition in the present.

This confession is important not just because it candidly discloses to the reader the tradition from which this study emanates. It also reveals something of my conception of theology. Principally it highlights the fact that in theology one speaks from a tradition. One does not begin from scratch. One inevitably stands on the intellectual shoulders of one's predecessors. This is a liberating discovery. It makes one aware of the humanity of the task, encourages a sense of debt and gratitude to others and brings to mind the diverse ingredients that are involved in theological judgement. The theological past is an inescapable dimension of the theological present; we go forward into the future not just out of the past but through it. This does not mean that things do not change. What it does mean is that tradition is of enormous significance. As one writes in the present one is related to a long line of predecessors who have helped to shape the questions and concepts that inform one's critical judgement. Of course new questions arise and new concepts are forged but these do not arrive out of nowhere. They too are shaped and in part determined by a history and a tradition that precedes them.

The proposals set forth in this study have been shaped by my past. They arise out of sympathetic and critical interaction with the Evangelical tradition within which I came to faith. They are motivated by a concern to preserve what is rich and true in that tradition and by a desire to express and develop that tradition in a way that is suitable and relevant to our day. They are an attempt to provide an account of divine inspiration that will be intelligible for today and yet also an expression of the classical Evangelical heritage in theology.

This latter claim will be a contested one. To many my main proposal will be too innnovative to be acceptable as a contribution to the Evangelical heritage. It is this issue that I want to discuss in this chapter. By attending to it I hope to set forth the contours of the Evangelical heritage as I see it and show how it relates to the content of the present proposals.

Postscript

At the outset let it be realized that my proposals do involve a departure from the orthodoxy of the recent past in Evangelical circles. Indeed it was dissatisfaction with the recent past that led me to think afresh about inspiration. So there is no denying that my position involves innovation. But the question that arises then is this: how far does it involve departure from the Evangelical tradition as a whole? Or to put the same issue in different words: how far can I claim continuity with the Evangelical tradition as it stretches back beyond the more recent past to figures like John Wesley and the great Reformers?

Everything depends on how we interpret the two key terms in the question. Given a proper and broad understanding of what continuity is and what the Evangelical tradition is, there can be no objection to the claim that my proposal is essentially Evangelical in character. Conversely, the objection under review arises from an improper and restrictive understanding of these key themes. It is because there is a narrow conception of what continuity is and what the Evangelical tradition has been that restrictive limits are set or what is to count as an adequate expression of that same tradition in the present. We can only break loose from this by developing a deeper and more realistic understanding of the complex continuity that is a necessary feature of our relationship with a rich and diverse past.

Evangelicals have too readily embraced a simplistic model of their relationship to the past. It is very tempting to see oneself as merely repeating what has been affirmed in the past. No more fitting illustration of this is to be found than the Princeton theologian, Charles Hodge. Speaking on the bi-centennial anniversary of Princeton Seminary he claimed: 'I am not afraid to say that a new idea never originated in this seminary.'[1] As we have seen, Evangelicals have pressed this especially forcefully in regard to the doctrine of inspiration. They have argued that they are simply repeating what the Church Universal has always believed prior to the rise of modern critical scholarship. Continuity had been interpreted as simply the repetition of what the Church has always believed everywhere.

There is a winning simplicity about this, for it is good to

feel so much at one with the saints and scholars of the past. Alas, it is an illusion to think that this is entirely possible. It is just not feasible to have this kind of total continuity with the past. Things are too relative to lend support to this extreme position. History is too rich and diverse for there to be no change. As a result we cannot be content merely to repeat what has been asserted in the past.

This is borne out by the very development of the standard account of inspiration. As we noted, it is not just a repetition of what was believed in the past. To be sure, the idea of inerrancy was carried over from an earlier generation. But even this does not guarantee that the precise content of the older view is maintained. Much depends on how one understands the concept of inerrancy adopted. Especially important at this point is the question of the criteria of inerrancy. Do we rely on our standards or do we rely on the standards available to the original writer? The gap here could be enormous, with the result that the actual continuity involved could be quite slim. The original agreement might then turn out to be purely verbal and superficial. What began as repetition could end as repudiation.

In fact the last generation of Evangelicals did repudiate central tenets of the previous era, for they vehemently rejected any talk of dictation. In this case there was no exact repetition of the past, even though the concept of dictation lingered on to take its revenge on the theories of those who rejected it. Those committed to the standard orthodoxy are in no position to insist on exact continuity with the past, for they do not practise it themselves.

Besides, they were innovators in a more positive sense. In reaction against the rise of biblical criticism they retreated to an account of inspiration that confined it in a very exclusive way to the original autographs. We can, in fact, actually date when this occurred. It occurred in 1879 in a book by A. A. Hodge.[2] At this point the continuity with the past is clearly broken. It is also broken in the kind of emphasis and status given to the doctrine of inspiration. Somehow it was isolated as of crucial significance for the whole of theology. Everything was made to stand or fall by it. Moreover adherence to it was made the badge of Evangelical respectability. All this goes beyond the more balanced and well-proportioned rôle that the doctrine enjoys in some earlier theologies of inspiration. The current orthodoxy on inspiration is not then as a matter of fact a mere repetition of earlier views in the Evangelical tradition. Nor can it be so as a matter of principle. The Evangelical tradition on inspiration is just too diverse to be acceptable wholesale. To believe it all would be akin to believing the proverbial six impossible things before breakfast. It cannot be done.

We can understand why this is so when we make a brief foray into the history of the Evangelical tradition. Unfortunately we do not have a definitive account of this tradition from a theological point of view. Some have begun to piece together the story, inspired in part by its recent rise to prominence especially in America. Sadly we are still saddled with the myths and prejudices that surround the topic. Evangelicals have themselves too readily accepted the picture drawn up by those outside the tradition who have failed to explore its foundations with sympathy and historical caution.

The Evangelical tradition has come to prominence in at least three different periods of Protestantism. As Donald Dayton has pointed out, the term 'Evangelical is associated with the Reformation, with the Evangelical revivals of the eighteenth and nineteenth centuries, and with Fundamentalism.[3] Any responsible account of the tradition must come to terms with the major thrusts of these movements. They have much in common and yet are not exactly the same. Let us dwell briefly on each of them.

At the time of the Reformation the term 'evangelical' simply described the emerging Protestant movement, especially its Lutheran wing. The central doctrine was the doctrine of justification by faith, founded and developed in the great *solus* slogans: *sola scriptura, solus Christus, sola gratia*. Here 'evangelical' simply means Protestant, as is reflected by the German usage of the word 'evangelisch' today. This usage is quite widespread in different parts of the world.

Next comes the period of the great Evangelical revivals, associated principally although not exclusively with John

Wesley and the Methodists. Here the main emphasis is on conversion and new life in Christ, on evangelism and on the renewal of the Church. Within it there is also a powerful impulse towards applying the gospel to life enshrined in the concern for holiness and perfect love. How far this actually worked its way into life is a mater of dispute. In this context the term 'evangelical' is associated with personal religious experience of forgiveness and renewal.

The last period lies closer to hand. The term 'evangelical' is also associated with the acrimonious controversy that raged in America in the early decades of the twentieth century. That controversy is known as the Fundamentalist–Modernist controversy and revolved around the extent to which the Church should accommodate itself to the new learning that had developed in the fields of science and history. The Fundamentalists strenuously opposed change, fearing that the substance of the faith was being lost in the rush to be relevant and up to date. As used in relation to this period 'evangelical' basically means conservative or orthodox.

It is this last period that many think of when they use the word 'evangelical'. Evangelicals are in fact referred to as 'conservative Evangelicals', a phrase that would be unintelligible were it not for the emergence of Fundamentalism as one of the key conservative forces in recent years of theology. Most people are still tempted to identify the Evangelical tradition with Fundamentalism, despite the fact that sporadic efforts have been made to distinguish the two. The latter can be seen most prominently in the efforts of those who desire to distance themselves from it without going the way of classical liberalism or contemporary radicalism. They do this by calling themselves 'Evangelicals' or 'neo-Evangelicals'. This distancing focuses especially on the quietist or politically reactionary dimension to Fundamentalism. Thus the call went out for Evangelicals to concern themselves with the social implications of the Gospel in contrast to its neglect in the first decades of this century. This issue is no longer debated on the level of principle; the discussion has moved on to the question of method and practice. As a result of these developments the term

'Evangelical' is sometimes used to identify the progressive wing of Fundamentalism.

These extremely important changes must not be allowed to blind us from seeing two salient facts. The first is that the doctrine of Scripture associated with much recent Evangelical theology is for the most part that of Fundamentalism. On this there has been little progress. The link at this point is Warfield. It was he who provided Fundamentalism with its theory of inspiration and it is he who stands behind the standard orthodoxy among Evangelicals at present. In this area many Evangelicals are far from progressive; they are extremely conservative in their desire to preserve the beliefs of the late nineteenth century. Indeed if anything they can be more rigid than the original Fundamentalists, for the latter happily accepted James Orr as a fellow-traveller, despite the fact that he rejected inerrancy.

The second fact we must keep in view is that the Evangelical tradition stretches back much further than the early years of our own century. The earlier periods of the Reformation and the great revivals cannot be ignored. It is to these that many now turn as their paradigms or models for the Evangelical tradition. This is my own position. It must not be taken to imply that Fundamentalism is rejected *in toto*. Far from it, for there is much to be learnt from this period of the past. But it does mean that there are values in the older traditions that are lacking in that era. This is especially so with regard to the doctrine of Scripture.

The values I have in mind are not to be found on the surface of the earlier traditions of the Evangelical heritage. If one looks merely to the surface one is likely to find commitment to some form of dictation. Consider a key figure like John Wesley. Various comments in his *Explanatory Notes upon the New Testament* clearly suggest that he believed in dictation. Thus his comment on John 19:24 has this to say about the writer of Psalm 22: '. . . in this scripture, as in some others the prophet seems to have been thrown into a preternatural ecstacy, wherein, personating the Messiah, he spoke barely what the Spirit dictated, without any regard to himself.'[4] As one expects from a Fellow of Lincoln College who taught logic, Wesley elsewhere drew the obvious inference from this when he insisted that there can be no falsehood in the Bible. 'If there be any mistakes in the Bible, there may as well be a thousand. If there be one falsehood in that book it did not come from the God of truth.'[5] *Prima facie* it might look therefore as if Wesley can have no value for today in our understanding of Scripture, for it looks as if he held an unbiblical and unfounded theory of dictation.

However, I suggest that this is to look to the surface of Wesley's theology of Scripture. In actual fact there are other concerns operating at a deeper level that are of the utmost importance. There are at least three of these.

The first concerns Wesley's openness to inductive considerations. Whatever he may have said in theory about lack of mistakes in the Bible, it is clear that when he actually studies it, he is prepared to admit that errors exist. Thus in his comment on Matt. 1:1, he accepts that an error may have been transmitted through the sources relied on by the writer. Indeed he even suggests that it would have been inappropriate to correct the mistake at issue. In this admission Wesley is at one with the great Irish commentator on early Methodism, Adam Clarke.[6] Both are therefore open in principle to examine Scripture as it stands; they are prepared to face inductive evidence from the content of the Bible before them. That this does not find its way back into Wesley's theory of inspiration is due, in my judgement, to the fact that he was not unduly concerned to work out a rounded account of inspiration *per se*. Other concerns absorbed his attention so that much of what he says about inspiration is tossed off as an aside rather than developed in the context of a full-dress theory of the Bible. What matters at this point is that he was prepared to face the fact that Scripture does contain falsehood in its details.

The second concern of Wesley that is of abiding significance is his focus on the actual purpose of Scripture. For him Scripture is primarily religious and spiritual in its nature and effects. Its purpose is to expound and make clear the mind of God in those things relevant to our relationship with him. The implication of this is that it is not Scripture's fault if it is time-bound in what it has to say on matters that are not central to salvation. To expect this is to miss that the Bible is first and foremost a means of grace. Adam Clarke put this point as follows: 'Inspiration was given to the holy men of old that they might be able to write and proclaim *the mind of God* in the things which concern the *salvation* of men.'[7]

This emphasis on the theological and salvific purpose of Scripture was central to the Reformers and those who came after them. For them too the Bible is principally a religious book with a divine message. Thus Samuel Rutherford, a key figure in the framing of the Westminster Confession, contends that Scripture is our rule 'not in things of Art and Scienc, as to speake Latine, to *demonstrate conclusions of Astronomie*'. According to Rutherford the Bible is not authoritative in these areas. 'But it is our Rule 1 in fundamentals of salvation.'[8] This emphasis is carried through to the Reformed tradition of today in the work of the Dutch theologian G. C. Berkouwer, who goes to some lengths in discussing the time-bound aspect of the content of Scripture. It is also picked up by the American Wesleyan scholar, John Oswalt. He puts the matter thus:

> . . . it is inappropriate to make the Bible the last word on matters relating to the physical sciences. Its purpose is not to express abstract scientific fact. Its purpose is to confront men and women in their own lives with the reality of a God who cannot be manipulated and yet can be trusted. In other words, its purpoose is to convey spiritual truth in concrete relationally-oriented terms. Since matters pertaining to the physical sciences are more or less peripheral to the Bible's major purpose, we ought not to take it as a text-book in those areas.[9]

The third area of great significance in Wesley's approach to the Bible is related to the rôle he is prepared to give to reason and experience in his theology as a whole. The Bible for Wesley is not the sole locus of authority in theology. To be sure it is pivotal and crucial; but it does not exclude the judicious appeal to reason and experience. This means that the foundations of Wesley's theology are manifold. Everything is not built on one pillar so that if minor cracks appear here or there in it the whole house is liable to fall. Rather he can appeal to wider rational and experiential considerations to back up his theological commitments.[10]

This has significant implications for an Evangelical

approach to the Bible in our day. First, it opens up space for biblical criticism such as has developed with the rise of historical study of the Bible. Valid insights from the field of reason are to be welcomed, not rejected, and reason must surely include historical reason. Secondly, it suggests that we can draw on philosophical considerations in our attempts to formulate a credible theory of inspiration. We can be open rather than closed towards the insights of philosophy as Wesley himself was in his appeal to it in his natural theology. We can sum up this major concern thus: Christians subject themselves to grave danger if they 'despise or lightly esteem reason, knowledge, or human learning' in their approach to the Bible, for each of these is 'an excellent gift of God, and may serve the noblest purposes'.[11]

All these concerns – to take inductive considerations seriously, to attend to the central purposes of Scripture, to draw on the wider insights of reason and experience – have been incorporated in the proposals developed earlier. I claim a genuine continuity therefore with the Evangelical past. This is a continuity in depth, as opposed to a surface-continuity that merely repeats the shibboleths of the past. Besides, I have tried to come to terms with the developments that have occurred with the passing of time. Both these considerations invite us to go boldly beyond the standard orthodoxy of recent years. In doing so we can articulate the values of the Evangelical heritage and at the same time speak to the intellectual concerns of our own day.

The danger is that the Fundamentalist wing of the Evangelical tradition will ignore this whole depth-dimension of the past. Certainly in the past Fundamentalists have been very quick to repudiate those who do not hold to a strict doctrine of inerrancy. This may well happen now. My hope is that there will be sufficient honesty to acknowledge the diversity of our past, sufficient sensitivity to the problems that need to be faced, and sufficient security in our convictions about the supreme importance of Scripture for all sides to recognize the unity that binds the various members of the Evangelical family together. Given this recognition then there is good ground for guarded optimism about what lies ahead.

NOTES

Introduction

1. Zondervan, Grand Rapids, 1976.
2. Evangelical Press, Welwyn, 1978.
3. J. I. Packer, *'Fundamentalism' and the Word of God* (IVP, London, 1958), p. 80.
4. Packer (*Fundamentalism*, p. 95) says that inerrancy is not essential. However he continues to make use of the term and to stress its importance.
5. The importance of this tradition has been highlighted recently by Donald W. Dayton in his *Discovering an Evangelical Heritage* (Harper and Row, New York, 1976).
6. See Packer, *Fundamentalism*, p. 39.

Chapter One

1. On the Interpretation of Scripture', in *Essays and Reviews* (Longmans, London, 1861), p. 345.
2. B. B. Warfield, *The Inspiration and Authority of the Bible* (Presbyterian and Reformed Publishing Company, Philadelphia, 1970), p. 105.
3. Ibid., p. 106.
4. Quoted in John Warwick Montgomery, 'Whither Biblical Inerrancy?', *Christianity Today*, xxi (1977), 1142.
5. Louis Gaussen *'Theopnustia': the Plenary Inspiration of the Holy Scriptures* Passmore and Alabaster, London, 1888. Translated by David Scott; revised by B. W. Care.
6. Ibid., p. 27.
7. Charles Hodge, *Systematic Theology* (Scribner, New York, 1871), i, p. 170.
8. Ibid., p. 171.
9. *The Use of Scripture in Recent Theology* (SCM, London, 1975), p. 22.
10. Kenneth S. Kantzer, 'Evangelicals and the Inerrancy Question', *Christianity Today*, xxii (1978), 904.
11. Gaussen, *'Theopneustia'*, p. 327.
12. Ibid., p. 333.
13. *A Defence of Biblical Infallibility* (Presbyterian and Reformed Publishing Company, Philadelphia, 1967), p. 30. Pinnock may be open to a change of mind on this. However, I have seen no evidence to suggest that he has actually changed his position in any substantial way.

14. *The Origins of Fundamentalism* (Fortress Press, Philadelphia, 1968) p. 25.
15. *Théopneustie ou Inspiration plénière des saintes écritures* (Paris and London, 1842), p. c2.
16. Ibid., p. 93.
17. Op. cit., English Translation by David Scott, p. 128.
18. Ibid., p. 48.
19. *'Fundamentalism' and the Word of God*, p. 79.
20. One can do this, for example, by insisting that the Bible must have absolute authority and then argue that this kind of authority assumes inerrancy.
21. Quoted in Gilbert Kirby, *Too Hot to Handle* (Marshall, Morgan and Scott, London, 1978). p. 1.
22. Idem.
23. Op. cit., p. 87.
24. See G. Kirby, op. cit., p. 5.
25. *The New Evangelical Theology* (Marshall, Morgan and Scott, London, 1969), p. 65. My italics.
26. Op. cit., p. 47.
27. Ibid., p. 79. Cf. John Wenham's conclusion in his *Christ and the Bible* (IVP, London, 1972), p. 187. He sums up Christ's view thus: 'To him, what Scripture says, God says.'
28. Op. cit., p. 169.

Chapter Two

1. W. Sanday, *Inspiration* (Longmans, Green and Co., London, 1903).
2. Ibid., p. 2.
3. Ibid., p. 394.
4. Ibid., p. 394.
5. Ibid., p. 145.
6. Ibid., p. 394.
7. Ibid., p. 127.
8. See note 5 above.
9. Op. cit., p. 396.
10. Ibid., p. 440-441.
11. Ibid., p. 392.
12. Ibid., p. 400.
13. Ibid., p. 189.
14. Ibid., p. 268.
15. James Barr, *Fundamentalism* (SCM, London, 1977), p. 348, fn. 33.
16. R. P. C. Hanson, *The Attractiveness of God: Essays in Christian Doctrine* (SPCK, London, 1973), p. 12.
17. Sanday, op. cit., p. 399.
18. Hanson, op. cit., p. 11.
19. Ibid., p. 21.

20. See his *Inspiration and Revelation in the Old Testament* (Clarendon Press, Oxford, 1946).
21. Ibid., p. 196.
22. SCM, London, 1977.
23. See especially his *Old and New in Interpretation* (SCM, London, 1966), and *The Bible in the Modern World* (SCM, London, 1973).
24. Barr, *The Bible in the Modern World*, p. 112.
25. Ibid., p. 17.
26. Ibid., p. 17.
27. Ibid., p. 17-18.
28. Ibid., p. 131-132.
29. In this paragraph I have drawn on personal communication with Professor Barr.
30. See above fn. 27.
31. Barr has suggested this in personal communication.
32. Warfield, op. cit., p. 202, fn. 47.

Chapter Three

1. It would take me too far afield to defend this conception of religious language. I touch on the issue in 'Some Trends in Recent Philosophy of Religion', *The Theological Educator*, ix (1979), 93-102. See Richard Swinburne, *The Coherence of Theism* (Clarendon Press, Oxford, 1977), Part I, for an excellent treatment of this issue.
2. *The Justification of Religious Belief* (Macmillan, London, 1973), p. 19.
3. W. Sanday, op. cit., p. 88.
4. John Baillie, *The Idea of Revelation in Recent Thought* (Columbia University Press, New York, 1956), p. 111.
5. I touch on this issue in the chapter that follows. As already indicated I hope to take up the whole question of revelation on a future occasion.

Chapter Four

1. For an excellent summary in this area see Bernhard Lohse's *A Short History of Christian Doctrine* (Fortress, Philadelphia, 1966), pp. 217f.
2. For an introduction to this field see James A. Sanders, *Torah and Canon* (Fortress, Philadelphia, 1974).
3. This, of course, is only one aspect of the profound effect that the rise of historical criticism has had on Christian theology.
4. SCM, London, 1952.
5. See his 'Revelation', *The Encyclopedia of Philosophy*, ed. Paul Edwards (Macmillan, New York, 1967), pp. 189-91; and his *Philosophy of Religion* (Prentice Hall, Englewood Cliffs, 1963), ch. 5. See also John Baillie, *The Idea of Revelation in Recent Thought* (Columbia University Press, New York, 1956).

6. Hick, 'Revelation', p. 190.
7. Paul Helm, 'On non-natural Revelation', unpublished.
8. These examples are furnished by Wright in G. Ernest Wright and Reginald Fuller, *The Book of the Acts of God* (Penguin, Harmondsworth, 1957), p. 190.
9. Rom. 1: 20.
10. Jean-Jacques Rousseau, *Emile* (Dent, London 1974), p. 245.
11. Ibid., p. 239.
12. In actual fact, as the appeal to Jesus is still an appeal to events in history, there is little difference in principle in this appeal to events in the history of Israel.
13. B. Albrektson, *History and the Gods* (Gleecup, Lund, 1967). Also of importance is the contribution of James Barr: see especially 'Revelation through history in the Old Testament and in Modern Theology', *Interpretation*, xvii (1963), 193-205.
14. Albrektson, op. cit., p. 122.
15. Ibid., p. 119. Cf. James Barr in *Old and New in Interpretation* (SCM, London, 1966), p. 23: 'Ultimately the emphasis upon the acts done by God in history rests upon an appeal to the actual forms of the Old Testament tradition. But we cannot have the emphasis upon the acting God unless we also have emphasis on the speaking God. One aspect of the form makes no sense without the other.'
16. Albrektson, op. cit., p. 122.
17. See 1 Cor. 1, 2; Gal. 1.
18. *Christian Believing* (SPCK, London, 1976), p. 105.
19. Ibid., p. 106.
20. Ibid., p. 108.

Chapter Five

1. B. B. Warfield, *The Inspiration and Authority of the Bible* (Presbyterian and Reformed Publishing Company, Philadelphia, 1970), p. 120.
2. *Fundamentalism* (SCM, London, 1977), p. 74.
3. Hans Von Campenhausen, *The Formation of the Christian Bible* (Fortress Press, Philadelphia, 1972), p. 1f.
4. *The Making of Christian Doctrine* (Cambridge University Press, Cambridge, 1967), p. 46.
5. Von Campenhausen, op. cit., pp. 15-16.
6. Warfield, op. cit., p. 299.
7. Ibid., p. 300. My italics.
8. See, for example, Psalm 119.

Postscript

1. Quoted in J. Gresham Machen, *A Biographical Memoir* (Westminster Theological Seminary, Philadelphia, 1954), p. 62.
2. See Ernest Sandeen, *The Origins of Fundamentalism* (Fortress Press, Philadelphia, 1968), p. 14. fn. 40.
3. 'Whither Evangelicalism? The Holiness Heritage Between Calvinism and Wesleyanism', unpublished paper read at the Sixth Institute of Methodist Theological Studies in Oxford.
4. *Explanatory Notes upon the New Testament* (Epworth, London, 1941), p. 383.
5. *Journal*, vi, 117.
6. See his *Commentary* (Thomas Tegg and Son, London, 1837), v, 36-7.
7. Ibid., vi, 1161.
8. Quoted in Jack Rogers, *Confessions of a Conservative Evangelical* (Westminster, Philadelphia, 1974), p. 99.
9. 'A Case for Biblical Authority', *The Asbury Seminarian*, xxxii (1977), 11-12.
10. This is not the place to defend Wesley's views. My aim is to highlight the diversity of opinion held by Evangelicals in the past.
11. John Wesley, *Works*, xi, 429.

INDEX

Albrektson, Bertil, 86
analogy, 61
Andrews, Edgar H., 1
Apostles, 41, 103
Aquinas, Thomas, 61
Asbury, Francis, 7
Augustine, 17
authority:
  as an argument for inerrancy, 31
  and inspiration, 74, 76–8
  and divine speaking, chapter 4
  crisis in, 76–8

Baillie, John, 68, 121
Barth, Karl, 32
Barr, James, 10, 46, 49–56
Berkouwer, G. C., 117

Canonical Criticism, 77
Clarke, Adam, 7, 116–17
Clement of Rome, 33
conceptual analysis, 57, 59–62
Conservative Evangelical, 12

Dayton, Donald, 119, 123
dictation, 3, 4, 28, 34, 36, 70–5, 115
divine action, 4, 59–61, 88–9
divine speaking, 87–9
  confused with divine inspiration, 36–7, 44, 60
  and authority, chapter 4
  cruciality of, 80–2
  in the Bible, 86–7

Erickson, Millard, 36
Evangelical tradition, 1, 6, 8, 12, Postscript
Evangelical revival, 113–14
exegesis, chapter 5

Fuller, Reginald, 122
fundamentalism, 114

Gaussen, Louis, 18, 23–7, 28–9, 32–4, 41, 45

Hanson, R. P. C., 47–8
Helm, Paul, 79–80
hermeneutics, 20–7
Hick, John, 79, 121
historical criticism, 10
  its impact on inerrancy, 5
  presuppositions of, 25
  compatible with inspiration, 69
  impact on the authority of the Bible, 77
Hodge, A. A., 111
Hodge, Charles, 19, 111
Holy Spirit, 43, 52–3

Illyricus, Matthias Flacius, 76
inerrancy, 2, 5, 10, 18–27, 30–5, 95, 99
infallibility, 5
inspiration:
  standard orthodoxy of recent years, 2
  intuition theory, 3
  illumination theory, 3
  dynamic theory, 3
  plenary or verbal theory, 3–4
  deductive approach to, 11–12, chapter 1
  inductive approach to, 11–12, chapter 2
  of original autographs, 28, 93–4, 112
  positive proposal, chapter 3
  paradigm case of, 63
  degrees of, 63
  a polymorphous concept, 64
  summary account of, 65
  in the present, 71–3
  biblical texts related to, chapter 5
  of the New Testament, 102–4

Index

intuition, 3, 48
Irenaeus, 33

Jesus, 95–102
Jones, Hywel R., 1
Jowett, Benjamin, 14

Kantzer, Kenneth, 119
Kelsey, David H., 20
Kirby, Gilbert, 120

Lampe, G. W. H., 87–9
law, 98–102
Lindsell, Harold, 1
Lohse, Bernard, 121
Luther, Martin, 7

Machen, J. Gresham, 123
Macquarrie, John, 6
Methodism, 115
miracle, 85
Mitchell, Basil, 61
Montgomery, John Warwick, 119
Murray, Ian, 1

original autographs, 93–4, 112
Oswalt, John, 117

Packer, J. I., 1, 4, 9, 16, 29, 37
Pinnock, Clark, 25–7, 119
Princeton Seminary, 28–9, 111
prophets, 41, 103

Reformation, 76, 113
revelation, 12–13, 49–50
  relation to inspiration, 66–7
  propositional, 73–4
  heilsgeschichtlich conception
    of, 78–90
  in creation, 83–4
  in human response, 89
Robinson, H. Wheeler, 10, 48–51, 56
Rogers, Jack, 123
Rousseau, Jean Jacques, 84
Rutherford, Samuel, 117

Sanday, William, 10, 41–7, 56
Sandeen, Ernest R., 28
Sanders, James A., 121
Spurgeon, C. H., 18
Swinburne, Richard, 121

tradition, 92
Trent, Council of, 76

von Campenhausen, Hans, 96, 101

Warfield, B. B., 1, 9, 15, 28, 34, 36,
  56–7, 93, 102–3
Wesley, Charles, 7
Wesley, John, 7, 8, 114–19
Wenham, John, 1
Westminster Confession, 117
Whitefield, George, 8
Wright, G. Ernest, 78